D0547731

The author's great-grandmother, who was a village nurse, sits holding a copy of *Pilgrim's Progress*. Many of the old sayings and rhymes in this book can be traced back to her.

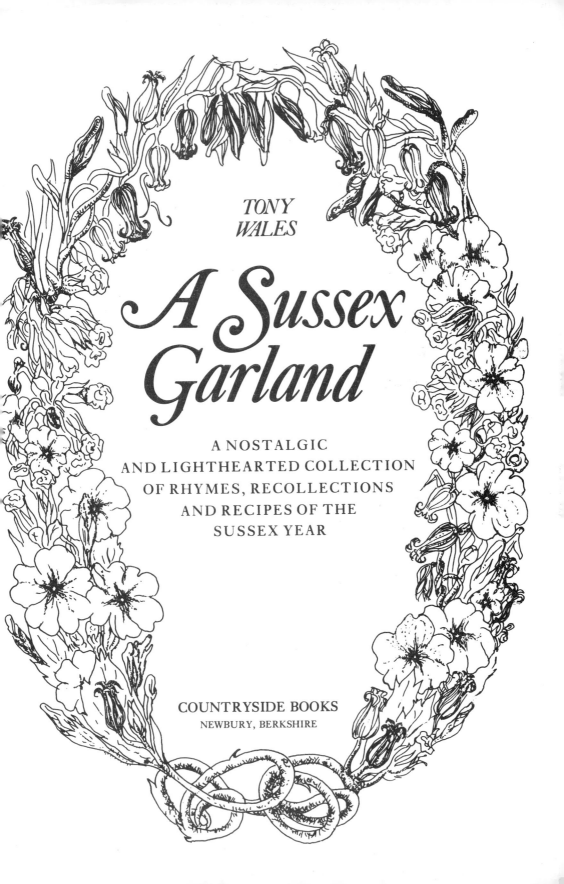

TONY
WALES

A Sussex Garland

A NOSTALGIC
AND LIGHTHEARTED COLLECTION
OF RHYMES, RECOLLECTIONS
AND RECIPES OF THE
SUSSEX YEAR

COUNTRYSIDE BOOKS
NEWBURY, BERKSHIRE

First Published
by Godfrey Cave Associates Ltd 1979
© Tony Wales 1979

This edition published
by Countryside Books 1986
Reprinted 1987

COUNTRYSIDE BOOKS
3 CATHERINE ROAD
NEWBURY BERKSHIRE

0 905392 64 7

The Cover Illustration is from an original painting
by Tommy Osborne

Produced through MRM (Print Consultants) Ltd., Reading
Printed in England by J. W. Arrowsmith Ltd., Bristol

Contents

Introduction 7
1. Wilfulness, Wassailing and Weather Lore 11
2. Fleas, Cuckoos and Cocks 27
3. May Day and Midsummer 43
4. Harvest Homes and Halloween 65
5. Guy Fawkes, Old Clem and Sussex Witches 87
6. Mince Pies, Mummers and Mistletoe 100
References and Bibliography 119
Index 123
Index to recipes 126

Acknowledgments

To THE MANY kind Sussex folk who have allowed me to share their memories and in particular to Mr C. W. Cramp, of Horsham, who provided me with many pictures. Also to Mrs C. Bacon, of South Harting; Mr E. Caplin and his father, both of Horsham; Mr W. Diplock, of Horsham; Mr H. Mousdell, of Ashington; Miss F. Woods, of Horsham; Mr J. Fyfield, of East Dean; Mr R. Ray, of Handcross; Mr G. Gutsell, of Hailsham; Mr W. Baker, of Bourne Hill, Horsham; Mr I. Park, of Burgess Hill; the Sussex Archaeological Society; the East Sussex County Library; the *West Sussex County Times*; Gellately-Norman Associates; and Picture Books Limited, of Brighton, for other material.

To the following, who contributed recipes: Dr A. W. Beatson, of Worthing; Mrs L. N. Candlin, of Brighton; Mrs E. Manvel, of Broadbridge Heath; Mrs L. Puttock, of Roffey; Mrs J. Shuttleworth, of Coventry; and Mrs E. Tucker, of Brighton; and to Mrs L. Wales, who checked the recipes.

To the many whose names I know not but who have kindly given me snippets of information about Sussex after my talks in different parts of the county. And, of course, to the members of my own family, who provided the initial impulse for this collection.

To the writers of the many Sussex books, pamphlets and newspaper reports from which I have gleaned so much over the years.

To Miss D. Bolton, who typed the final manuscript; to the Sussex Family History Group, which publicised my search for old Sussex photographs; and to Tommy Osborne, whose painting is reproduced on the cover.

I would, finally, like to remember many old Sussex friends who are no longer with us but who are mentioned or quoted in the text. A little of their wisdom lives on in these pages.

Introduction

ALTHOUGH I HAVE LINKED the material in this book to the seasons of the year, the link has sometimes been a little contrived. The real, underlying theme has been Sussex as it existed around seventy years ago. I have rather casually moved back, and occasionally forward, in time from this point, but the period shown in sharpest focus is the time of my mother's childhood, c. 1890–1900: before I was born, of course, but still not too long ago to come alive to many people who, like myself, have talked at length to older folk with good memories.

As we move towards the 1990s and, presumably, even greater materialism and dependence on technology, so many people's minds and hearts reach out to other, less soul-destroying influences. Nostalgia for times past may be unrealistic, but I do not feel that it can be harmful to ponder occasionally on times which were slower, perhaps easier to understand and undoubtedly more peaceful than the present day.

Thus, these glimpses of a Sussex in the main vanished, yet still lingering on in varying ways, are offered to those who care to stop and think about the past. They will not prevent the future, but at least in a tiny way they may help to make it a little more endurable.

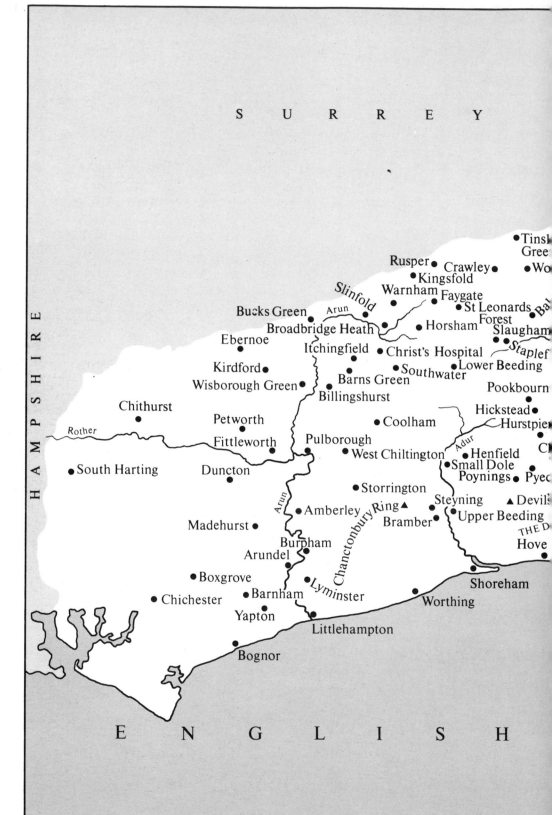

S U R R E Y

H
A
M
P
S
H
I
R
E

Tinsl
Gree

Rusper
Crawley
Wo
Kingsfold
Warnham
Faygate
Slinfold
Bucks Green
Arun
St Leonards
Ba
Forest
Broadbridge Heath
Horsham
Slaugham
Ebernoe
Itchingfield
Christ's Hospital
Staplef
Kirdford
Southwater
Lower Beeding
Wisborough Green
Barns Green
Pookbourn
Billingshurst
Hicksted
Chithurst
Coolham
Hurstpier
Rother
Petworth
Pulborough
Adur
Fittleworth
West Chiltington
Henfield
Cl
Duncton
Small Dole
South Harting
Storrington
Poynings
Pyec
Arun
Steyning
Devil
Amberley
Ring
Madehurst
Bramber
Upper Beeding
Chanctonbury
THE D
Burpham
Hove
Arundel
Boxgrove
Lyminster
Shoreham
Chichester
Barnham
Worthing
Yapton
Littlehampton
Bognor

E N G L I S H

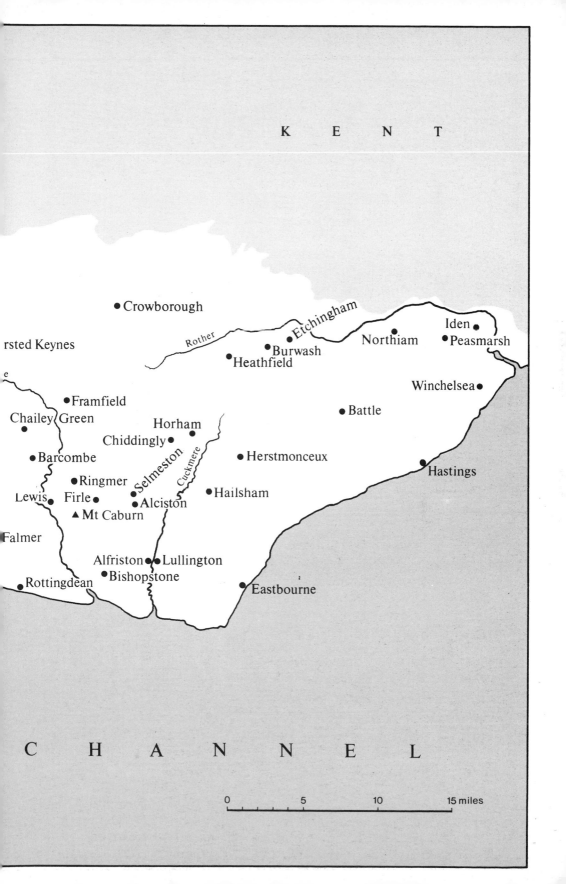

K E N T

Crowborough

Rother

Etchingham

Iden
Northiam
Peasmarsh

rsted Keynes

Burwash
Heathfield

Winchelsea

e

Framfield

Battle

Chailey Green

Horham

Barcombe

Chiddingly

Cuckmere

Herstmonceux

Selmeston

Ringmer

Hailsham

Lewis
Firle
Alciston

Hastings

▲ Mt Caburn

Falmer

Alfriston Lullington

Rottingdean
Bishopstone

Eastbourne

C H A N N E L

0   5   10   15 miles

Wilfulness, Wassailing and Weather Lore

PERHAPS THE tenacity of traditional lore in Sussex is due mainly to our characteristic obstinacy and dislike of change. Apart from those folk customs now extinct but still remembered, there are many still being pursued, either as part of an unbroken tradition or in modern revival.

These are accompanied by much other living folklore. Along with the modern methods of farming, many Sussex farmers still stick to the old weather rhymes and signs, for instance. Similarly, although we have the benefits of a modern health service, some people prefer the old remedies and cures. Space travel and all the trappings of modern technology are close at hand, but a part of our obstinate Sussex mind still refuses to discount completely the ancient beliefs and superstitions.

Like Christianity, which was late in reaching Sussex, the twentieth century and all that it stands for is still not wholly accepted by the real Sussex countryman or woman. There are still people who refuse to alter their clocks at 'daylight saving time' but instead prefer to remain an hour different to most other people during part of the year.

The Sussex character embraces slowness of speech, slowness to anger and a reluctance to accept changes. It can be neatly summed up in the jingle,

> *You may push and you may shuv,*
> *But I'm hemmed if I'll be druv!*

Miss Faith Woods has provided me with a longer poem which makes the point even more clearly. Many people seem to know the last stanza, incidentally, but I have been unable to find out any more about it, apart from the name of the author, Victor Cook.

> *Some folks as come to Sussex,*
> *They reckons as they know –*
> *A durn sight better what to do*
> *Than simple folks, like me and you,*
> *Could possibly suppose.*

But them as comes to Sussex,
They mustn't push and shove,
For Sussex will be Sussex,
And Sussex won't be druv!

Mus Wilfred come to Sussex,
Us heaved a stone at he,
Because he reckoned he could teach
Our Sussex fishers how to reach
The fishes in the sea,
But when he dwelt among us,
Us gave un land and luv,
For Sussex will be Sussex,
And Sussex won't be druv!

All folks as comes to Sussex
Must follow Sussex ways –
And when they've larned to know us well,
There's no place else they'll wish to dwell
In all their blessed days –
There ant no place like Sussex,
Until ye goos above,
For Sussex will be Sussex,
And Sussex won't be druv!

From the foregoing, you will begin to get the idea that Sussex folk hate to be rushed. My grandfather had a one-word reply to anyone who had the temerity to enquire when he would finish a job. Invariably, he would answer, 'Drackly' (directly), meaning not straight away but when he was good and ready.

My great-grandmother (my mother's grandmother) was a country nurse who walked the dark Sussex roads and lanes with only a candle lantern for company. It was said of her that she feared neither man nor beast. Her share of Sussex obstinacy obviously had a lot to do with this. My mother, also Sussex, used to tell of the time she was invited by her grandmother to her cottage for tea. A boiled egg was placed before the little girl, who asked for salt to put on it. Grandmother didn't have any salt and refused to go to a neighbour and borrow some. Equally obdurate, my mother refused to eat the egg without salt. Consequently, she went without her tea, but they both had the satisfaction of not having given in.

Family apart, there are many stories which illustrate what our enemies would term our 'pigheadedness' (although the Sussex country-dweller would scarcely consider this an insult, the useful pig being held in high regard).

Old Stephen Potter, a retired farmer who lived in New Street, Horsham, for

'We wunt be druv' – the old Sussex motto is admirable symbolised by this 'village parliament' of local worthies, photographed at Amberley in 1914.

The 'pigheadedness' of Sussex folk is even more pointedly suggested on this postcard, sent in 1910. In fact, the pig is a much-respected animal in Sussex and to be called pigheaded by no means the insult there that it might be elsewhere.

Have got as fat as a Sussex—

AND—

" wunt be druv " from Brighton.

R.F., E.

many years, was told by his family that he might no longer wear his round-frock, or smock, to chapel, as it was out of fashion. Rather than appear without his beloved smock, he gave up attending service from that day onwards. Similar stories concerning old men and their smocks are told in several parts of the county. In one, the central character has his smock hidden by his daughter before church time. Reluctantly, he leaves without it, but takes his coat off while he walks through the village, hoping that his cronies will conclude that he is in his shirtsleeves due to the heat.

Smocks lingered on in Sussex into the 1920s, when they were occasionally donned by bearers at a funeral. Now, any that remain are considered collector's items and are once again worn with pride on special occasions.

In spite of his deceptive slowness, it is very hard to 'put one across' the true Sussex countryman. I was told recently of a certain professional gentleman who had the habit of leaving his office at odd times during the afternoon and arriving home unexpectedly, in the hope of catching his gardener out in some misdeed. On one of these occasions he said to the gardener, in his usual gruff voice, 'I hope you are planting those potatoes well apart!' 'Y-yes,' replied the fellow, 's-some in your garden and s-some in m-mine!'

Another example of the Sussex man's contempt for misplaced authority lies in the story of the farmworker who visited a fair at Crawley, looking for employment for the coming year. A certain farmer approached him and told him to go and get his 'character' (a reference). Later in the day, they met again and the farmer enquired, 'Have you got your character?' 'No,' said the man, 'but I got yourn and I ain't coming!'

However, some bosses of extra strong will could overawe even their Sussex workfolk. Mr Catt, a farmer at Bishopstone, near Lewes, kept both his family and workforce in their places. At a particular harvest supper, one man, somewhat carried away, had the courage to say to him, 'Give us yer hand, Sir! I love ye, I love ve, Sir! But I'm damned if I beant afraid of ye, though.'

But most working folk were more sure of themselves. George Goodyer, of Burpham, a carpenter, looked at a wooden building he had just finished and said, 'It may not be much to look at but, by jingo, it's hellfire strong!'

The late Lawrie Graburn, also of Burpham, wrote under the name of Newall Duke (Duke was his mother's family name) and told many tales of his Duke relations. One concerned Mr Blake Duke, of Lyminster. Warned by his doctor not to drink more than one glass of port a day, Blake had a special large-size tumbler made which held as much as a full bottle.

An apt example of Sussex stubbornness is provided by the story of the old man who declared his intention to eat his old pig after it finally died of old age. Some time after, a friend met him and asked if he had indeed eaten the animal.

'Yes, I et im,' came the reply. 'It took me a year to do it, but I et im.'

The Sussex countryman has never been inclined to divulge more

A Sussex man wears a proud family possession – a smock, or round frock. Smocks were common in Sussex up to the 1920s (though by that time confined mostly to bearers at funerals). The building in the background is Cobb's Mill, on the upper reaches of the Adur, near Hurstpierpoint. Built in the nineteenth century, it was in use up to 1966. In the days when it was commonplace to work round the clock, the miller ('Old Man Packham') would not permit Sunday working, so the mill stopped for twenty-four hours every Saturday at midnight.

Smocks are much in evidence at this village 'club day', photographed around 1908. For 'club days', see chapter 3.

information than is absolutely necessary. Writing in 1922, Miss Kensett, of Horsham, tells of walking through St Leonard's Forest, from Slaugham to Horsham, and coming to a fork in the road. She asked an old fellow who overtook her, 'Does this road go to Horsham?' He told her it did, but himself took the alternative route. When she came to where the two roads met, he was almost out of sight ahead of her. His destination had been the same, but he had taken the shorter road, leaving her to her own devices.

Henry Burstow, the old Horsham cobbler, singer and bell-ringer, always helped to ring the bells of the parish church of St Mary the Virgin, in the Causeway, but never stopped to attend a service. When the vicar remonstrated with him, the old man answered, 'I fetches 'em in, and I leaves you to send 'em away.' To his credit, the vicar respected him for his honesty and even defended him against those critics who failed to appreciate his peculiar Sussex qualities.

Another story from Miss Kensett goes back to the time when the town hall, in Market Square, was open underneath, with the main building supported on pillars. Carters bringing their horses and carts into town used to stay at the Anchor pub, then also in Market Square, stabling their horses in the yard but leaving the carts in the square, ready for the morning. One particular carter was unpopular with the locals and when he left his cart in the accustomed place, some youngsters decided to get it under the Town Hall. To do so, they had to take off the wheels and drag the cart in by brute force; they then replaced the wheels. When the carter came for his cart in the morning, he spent a long time trying to work out not only how to get his cart out but how it had got in there in the first place.

Even our Sussex roads are stubborn: it used to be said of a difficult task that it was 'like a bit of Sussex road'.

A sombre little story to end on. It tells of an old Horsham couple who were to be sent to the workhouse in Crawley Road (known even up to my childhood simply as 'The Union'). This was in the days when married couples who were unfortunate enough to end up in the workhouse were separated for all but a short period each day. Rather than face this separation, after the best part of a lifetime together, they walked hand in hand into Warnham Mill pond . . .

◇ ◇ ◇

At the beginning of JANUARY, 1977, an ancient New Year ritual was revived. The Broadwood Morris Men, from Horsham – named after Lucy Broadwood, of Rusper, the famed collector of folk songs – wassailed the apple trees at Redlands Farm, Kirdford. Flaming torches lit the scene as the men chanted and paraded round the trees, watched by about eighty onlookers.

Wassailing, charming, whostling or howling the fruit trees is a custom of unknown age, but undoubtedly very old indeed. It was usually enacted around Christmastime, sometimes on Boxing Day, but more often on 6 January, the

Skaters on Warnham Mill Pond, February 1912. I can remember being taken there by my father when I was very small and being amazed at the uncharacteristically abandoned behaviour of all these grownups on the ice – and excited by the smell of hot chestnuts from a stall on the bank. Following a number of accidents, skating on the Pond was discouraged. In the photograph, boys from the Blue Coat School of Christ's Hospital can be seen, in their distinctive uniforms.

'February Filldyke' – floods at Bramber in 1904.

feast of the Epiphany. Wassailing the trees meant to wish them good health in the coming year and was accompanied by various rituals intended to drive away any evil spirits that might be lurking in the branches. Possibly these rituals had their beginnings in the pre-Christian nature religions.

In Sussex, the wassailers were most often called howlers, or the Howling Boys. The custom was for a group of men and boys to assemble in the orchard with pails of ale or cider. Various songs or rhymes were sung, accompanied by the sound of a cow horn (possibly an explanation for the name 'howling boys'). Guns loaded with powder were then fired into the branches of the trees. (In 1977, they used a muzzle-loading 12 bore shotgun dating from 1830.) Toasts were drunk to the trees and toasted bread put into the branches. Sometimes, the actual type of apple was specified in the rhymes. In some cases, the wassailers would be the owners of the fruit trees, with their family and friends. In others, a band of men would go from house to house, offering to 'whostle' the trees and expecting to be paid for doing so, rather like carol singers.

Here are two of the rhymes used:

> *Here's to thee, old apple tree,*
> *May'st thou bud, may'st thou blow.*
> *Hats full, caps full, bushel, bushel bags full,*
> *And my pockets full, too.*

> *Here stands a good old apple tree.*
> *Stand fast, root ; bear well, top.*
> *Every twig, apples big,*
> *Every bough, apples enou'.*
> *Hats full, caps full, four and twenty sacks full.*

The custom was carried on in Sussex until late in the nineteenth century, continuing longer in some villages than in others. Probably the last place in which it continued without a break was Duncton. A photograph taken in about 1897 shows Richard (Spratty) Knight, who was the Duncton captain. The photograph shows Spratty under an apple tree, wearing a suit made of some bright, flowered material, a string of apples round his neck and a large hat, decorated with apples, on his head. His wife stands beside him, holding a cake, a plate and a jug. William Knight, the vice-captain, also wears a hat decorated with apples.

Wassailing the apple trees lingered on in Sussex until about 1920, then died; but it was revived a few years ago by the Chanctonbury Ring Morris Men at Hailsham, followed by further revivals in the late seventies by both the Chanctonbury and Broadwood Men.

Long may they continue.

⌀ ⌀ ⌀

THE ROYAL SUSSEX COUNTY HOSPITAL, BRIGHTON.

POUND DAY, 1917.

Please keep up the good old custom and send your Valentine in money or kind on WEDNESDAY, FEBRUARY 14th, to the Board Room of the Hospital, or the Reception Room at the Hove Town Hall, between 10 a.m. and 6 p.m.

The Hospital will be open to Donors during these hours.

Putting an old custom to good use. The Royal Sussex Hospital – at the time heavily burdened with military patients, 100 of its 264 beds being reserved for war wounded – could expect to receive a fair proportion of its income from Pound Day donations. Pound Day, 1917, realised the then handsome sum of £364. Pound Days were one of many ways in which the old voluntary hospitals raised money.

Our Sussex forests were not always quiet retreats. Once, they resounded to the throb of the iron foundries – and then there were the charcoal burners, like this group in Balcombe Forest, around 1907. One wonders if they felt as benign as they look at having their lunch disturbed – perhaps even delayed – by the attentions of the photographer.

Rather less well known than the wassailing of the apple trees was the wassailing of the beehives in some villages.

Beekeepers know that they must treat their charges with respect. In the past, and perhaps to some extent even today, the custom has been to 'tell the bees' of any important happenings within the family circle. At the time of a death, the bees had to be told and the hives draped with black crepe. After a wedding, the bride was expected to visit the bees while still in her wedding dress.

Failure to observe these conventions could result in the bees taking their leave. An old lady who spoke to me after one of my Women's Institute talks said that she remembered being invited to 'come and meet the bees' as her first duty whenever, as a young girl, she visited an old friend of the family.

Little lore connected with wassailing of the hives appears to have survived, but we do have a rhyme:

> *Bees, O Bees of Paradise, does the work of Jesus Christ,*
> *Does the work which no man can,*
> *God made bees, and bees made honey,*
> *God made man, and man made money,*
> *God made great men to plough and to sow,*
> *God made little boys to tend the rooks and crows,*
> *God made women to brew and to bake,*
> *And God made little girls to eat up all the cake,*
> *Then blow the horn.*

The peculiar efficacy of bee stings in the treatment of rheumatism may appear to some as a relatively modern form of alternative medicine, but old beekeepers discovered their particular immunity to rheumatic pains a long time ago. It was not unknown for patients to submit to systematic stinging in order to gain relief, and while some city doctors may have looked on this as superstition, those closer to country things knew that there was more to it than that.

There is also a vast lore, some of it fancy but most of it fact, surrounding honey and its medicinal properties. Within many people's memories, it formed the basis of home-made cough mixtures and throat medicines. Undoubtedly, there is more to the humble bee than just a buzz and a sting.

◇ ◇ ◇

Up until my mother's youth, superstitions relating to one's future wife or husband were very popular. One promised that if a girl sat across a gate or style and looked at the first moon after New Year's Day, she would see the likeness of her future spouse. She had to be quite alone and, when the moon appeared, to recite this rhyme:

> *All hail to thee, Moon, all hail to thee.*

Sussex celebrations of different kinds. *Above:* the carter's pride – a wedding procession at Ringmer prepares to set off for church in the days before limousines. The wagon would be covered if it rained. The decorations on the horses took many hours to make.

A Foresters' parade along the Brighton road at Horsham in 1881. The musicians could not afford uniforms, but their hats gave them a certain dignity. One of the banners reads, 'Train up a child in the way he should go'.

I pray thee, good Moon, reveal to me
This night who my husband must be.

25 January (St Paul's Day) was once considered important if you wanted to know how successful the coming year was to be:

If Paul's Day be bright and clear,
We'll have good luck all through the year

2 FEBRUARY, Candlemass Day, was also a day which augured either well or ill for the months to come, but in this case it was the weather which was being forecast, not personal fortunes. If the weather was fine on Candlemass Day, then winter continued for a while longer. If, however, it was rainy, then winter came to an end.

14 February is still celebrated as St Valentine's Day, with special dances and parties and, of course, the much commercialised custom of Valentine cards. Traditionally, it was supposed to be the day on which the birds took their mates.

When my mother and her sisters were in their teens, much amusement was caused by the belief that the first person of the opposite sex you saw in the morning was your Valentine for the coming year. All sorts of tricks were resorted to to ensure that the right person appeared at the right time.

27 February was the date of a less pleasant custom, once popular in the Southwater area. This was the annual hare hunt, in which the hares were

25 GUINEAS
REWARD.

Henfield Prosecuting Society.

WHEREAS some evil disposed Person or Persons, did, in the Night of Tuesday, the 8th Instant, break open the Stable on Furzefield Farm, in the Parish of Shermanbury, in the occupation of Mr. THOMAS PAGE, and maliciously CUT OFF and carry away

THE HAIR
FROM THE

TAILS OF 3 CART HORSES
the property of the said THOMAS PAGE.
A REWARD OF
FIVE GUINEAS

will be given to any Person or Persons giving Information of the Offender or Offenders, so that he or they may be Convicted thereof; such Reward to be paid by the Treasurer of the said Society, immediately after such Conviction.

THOMAS COPPARD, Clerk.

HORSHAM, 9th MAY, 1838.

A FURTHER REWARD OF

20 GUINEAS

will be paid on such Conviction as aforesaid, by me

THOMAS PAGE.

Printed by Charles Hunt, West Street, Horsham.

Was this poster of 1838 serious? Certainly, the Henfield Prosecuting Society, formed in 1822 to assist the police in combating a spate of lawlessness which followed the Napoleonic Wars, was serious enough. It was one of many such societies formed in Sussex towns and villages about this time. (*Photograph: University of Reading Museum of English Rural Life.*)

Now well known as one of the post-Second World War 'new towns', Crawley was once a busy little country town on the London–Brighton road. The wide High Street was the site for markets and fairs, providing quite a hazard for through traffic! This picture was taken in 1914.

Winter throws huge seas even on to the usually placid shores of Sussex and many seaside towns in the county have noble records for rescue by lifeboat in the most appalling conditions. Launching the lifeboat (*below*, at Eastbourne, around 1910) was an operation requiring many hands; but there were always plenty of townsfolk there to help.

hunted and killed and then eaten in the evening at the Cock Inn, Southwater. This was still going on in the 1860s but had died out by the end of the century.

⌒ ⌒ ⌒

Sussex mud is something whose quality the traveller soon comes to appreciate. It was called 'Loving Mud', because 'it do cling so'. In January, the mud is called 'January butter' and it is considered lucky to bring it into the house (although whether the housewife would agree is debatable). The month following was known as 'February Filldyke' (a 'dyke' in Sussex meaning a ditch), so obviously the first two months of the year were among the muddiest. A writer in 1751 wrote that 'Sussex oxen, swine and all other animals have extra long legs, because their muscles become stretched through pulling their legs out of the mud.' In the seventeenth century, a tariff for coaches announced uniform tolls for everywhere except Sussex, as the roads there were so bad that they could be only partly used in winter. In 1703, the King of Spain took six hours to travel the last nine miles to Petworth, and in 1749 Horace Walpole wrote, 'If you love good roads, never go into Sussex.'

There are several stories about our mud. One, evidently true, tells of the lady of the manor who, trying to get to church one Sunday, failed with her horses and so had the farm oxen, normally only used for ploughing, hitched up to her carriage, arriving at church on time if with rather less than her usual dignity.

━━━━━

Puddings

It used to be said, 'Don't go into Sussex, or they will make you into a pudding.' Certainly we are very fond of our puddings and we make them both sweet and savoury and out of almost anything edible. Although they are eaten right through the year, winter seems a good time to think about dishes with names like Hasty Pudding and Acres Pudding.

ACRES PUDDING
So called because, it was said, Sussex folk could eat it by the acre!

6 oz suet	*6 oz flour*
6 oz raisins	*¼ pint milk*

Mix ingredients together well and bake in a tin for 1 hour.

OLD–FASHIONED BREAD PUDDING
A useful way of using up stale bread, from a time when it was considered almost criminally wasteful to throw *anything* edible away.

½ lb stale bread	1 level tablespoon syrup
2 oz suet	1 egg
6 oz mixed dried fruit	½ level teaspoon bicarbonate of soda
2 oz brown sugar	3 tablespoons milk
1 level teaspoon mixed spice	
1 level teaspoon ground ginger	

Soak bread in water for 30 minutes. Drain and squeeze well. Beat to remove lumps. Add suet, mixed fruit, sugar, mixed spice, ginger, syrup and beaten egg. Blend mixture well. Dissolve bicarbonate of soda in milk and beat into mixture. Turn into square tin, well greased, and bake in the centre of oven at mark 4 for $1-1\frac{1}{4}$ hours.

HASTY PUDDING

4 bay leaves	Salt
2 eggs	Butter
1 quart milk	Flour

Boil the bay leaves in the milk. Beat up the yolks of the eggs with salt and two or three spoonsful of the milk. Take out the bay leaves, mix the flour gradually into the milk with a wooden spoon until you have a thick mixture. Let this boil, stirring continually. Pour into a dish and stick butter in different parts.

(Published in *The Mistress of Stanton's Farm*, Marcus Woodward, 1938.)

BOLSTER or BLANKET PUDDING

Suet dough	Swedes
Lean bacon	Butter
Onion	Black pepper
Sage leaves	

Spread the suet crust with a mixture of lean bacon, chopped onions and a few crushed sage leaves. Fold into a blanket or bolster shape. Tie in a cloth and boil for about 2 hours. Serve with cooked swedes, mashed with butter and black pepper. (Sausage meat can be substituted for the bacon.)

The suet crust can also be cooked plain and eaten cold with cheese and raw onion between the folds.

MILITARY PUDDING

6 oz breadcrumbs	1 tablespoon ground rice
3 oz suet	1 lemon
3 tablespoons sugar	1 egg

Mix ingredients together with the grated rind of the lemon, the egg and the lemon juice. Pour into mould, which has been buttered and lined with stoned raisins. Steam for $2\frac{1}{2}$ hours.

(Published in *Sussex County Magazine*, vol. 10.)

RICE AND APPLE PUDDING

$\frac{1}{4}$ *lb rice*	*Nutmeg*
Milk	*Sugar*
1 egg	*Apples*
Cream	

Boil the rice in milk until it is both tender and as thick as you can stir. Add the egg and a few teaspoons of cream, nutmeg and sugar to taste. Peel and core enough apples to half fill a dish. Pour the rice over the apples and bake for 30 minutes.

(Published in *Sussex County Magazine*, vol. 10.)

SWIMMERS

Suet dough	*Brown sugar*
Butter	

Make a suet dough and shape into flat, round pieces about the size of a saucer. Drop into boiling water and cook quickly for about 20 minutes. To serve, break open the centre with a fork, put a dollop of butter and a spoonful of brown sugar on top.

Swimmers should be eaten immediately they are taken out of the saucepan.

SUSSEX PUDDING

1 lb strawberries	*1 pint milk*
$\frac{1}{4}$ *lb castor sugar*	$\frac{1}{2}$ *oz French gelatine*
$\frac{1}{2}$ *pint water*	$1\frac{1}{2}$ *oz sugar*

Cook strawberries with castor sugar and water until soft and rub through a sieve. Put milk, gelatine and sugar into saucepan and bring to the boil. Stir while boiling until gelatine is dissolved. Strain into a jug. Put the fruit pulp into a glass dish and pour the milk over just before it sets. Serve cold.

MACKEREL PUDDING

Suet dough	*Black pepper*
Mackerel (boned)	*Salt*
Belly of pork, cut into cubes	*Bay leaf*

Fill a pudding basin with the boned mackerel pieces and pork cubes. Season with pepper, salt and bay leaf. Cover with suet dough and cook like a steak-and-kidney pudding.

Fleas, Cuckoos
and Cocks

THERE ARE SEVERAL sayings connected with MARCH, the best-known being, of course, 'If March comes in like a lamb, it will go out like a lion.' Another is, 'March dust is worth a guinea a bushel', again relating to the strong winds proverbially associated with the period. Less well known is the saying, 'Eat winkles in March and it is as good as a dose of medicine.'

1 March is particularly connected with fleas in Sussex. The saying is, 'On the first of March, the fleas start jumping.' In West Sussex, we say, 'Never open your windows, or you will get a swarm of fleas in the house.' In East Sussex, they say, '*Always* open your windows, or you will get a swarm of fleas in the house.' Another version is, 'If from the fleas you would be free, on the first of March let all your doors and windows open be.'

This comes from West Sussex. In East Sussex, the final words are 'closed be'.

Whether you believe in the East or West Sussex admonitions, 1 March seems to be the day to start spring cleaning, by sweeping out the cracks of the doors and windows. No doubt fleas were once a very great 'irritation' to the good Sussex housewives.

If we are unlucky enough to have snow in APRIL, we say, 'The gates were left open at Crowborough Fair.' This is one of several sayings, all of equally obscure origin, connected with Sussex fairs.

Another fair is remembered on 14 April, 'Cuckoo Day' or 'Heffel Cuckoo Day' in Sussex. This was traditionally remembered as the day on which the old woman at Heathfield Fair released the first cuckoo of the year from her basket. No one seems to know the origin of the story, but it is widely quoted and known even in Surrey.

Many strange beliefs once centred around the cuckoo. It was held that cuckoos turned into hawks and stayed the winter, and that they could not call until they found some birds' eggs to suck. Even today, some store is set by hearing the first cuckoo, although it must be admitted that some early cuckoos may be good imitations by youngsters. The folk song, *The Cuckoo Is a Pretty Bird*, is well known in Sussex.

Shrove Tuesday was once associated in Sussex with cock throwing (throwing weighted sticks called 'libbets' at tethered cocks) and cock fighting. At Billingshurst, many people came from miles around for this 'sport' until, in 1804, the Reverend P. Evershed pinned a poem to his church door condemning the practice. To their credit, his parishioners then abandoned it. In the Brighton Lanes, the game was known as 'cock in the pot', but there it came to an end in 1780.

A happier custom also associated with the beginning of Lent was the start of the marbles and skipping season. This continued until Good Friday, when it culminated in a positive frenzy of skipping and marble playing all over the county.

Good Friday was known as either 'Long Rope (or Line) Day' or 'Marble Day'. The rope was used for skipping, which was not confined to children, adults also taking part, including Brighton fishermen and their families, using ropes made from Brighton hemp. The true significance of skipping has been lost, although legend has it that the ropes were in some way connected with the story of Judas hanging himself. Skipping originally had a magical significance and is certainly a very old tradition indeed, perhaps stretching back into pre-Christian days.

One place for Good Friday skipping was a large barrow, now part of Hove's Palmeira Avenue, where the skippers recited the rhyme, *Hey Diddle Diddle, Jump on the Bury*. The Downs were also popular for this purpose and Newhaven people used to walk over them to skip in front of the Rose Cottage inn at Alciston.

Other Good Friday games included skittles, on the Level at Brighton, and orange and egg rolling, at Shoreham, down Good Friday Hill. Hot cross buns were also eaten in Sussex, as elsewhere, to the common rhyme, *One a penny, two a penny*.

Brighton fishermen, who appear to have been staunch custodians of old customs, used to take hot cross buns to sea as good luck charms. It was also customary to retain some of each year's buns, which were said to keep hard and firm without going mouldy.

For those who preferred work to play, it was considered the correct thing to plant one's seed potatoes on Good Friday, but to abstain from other work. It was also said to be unlucky to throw any water outside.

But to return to the pastime for which Good Friday was particularly noted all over Sussex – marble playing – legend would have it that Good Friday marble playing was a survival of the casting of lots, by fives or knuckle bones, for Christ's garments. Again, we have no certain knowledge of how the custom began, but there is conclusive evidence that marble playing is a very old game.

Good Friday marble playing now survives in Sussex mainly at Tinsley Green – which is, in fact, half in Sussex and half in Surrey – and at Battle,

In Lent, boys played marbles (*above*, in West Chiltington), while both girls and boys had their hoops (*below*); the girls' hoops were made of wood, the boys' of iron. Children of every generation seem to know by instinct when the appropriate seasons arrive for outdoor games. Many of the sturdy villas typified in the picture below – taken at Rottingdean in 1906 – are still surviving. The photographer on this occasion seems to have got the villagers to pose a little less obviously than usual. The top picture is more typical – even the horse seems to be standing quite still, to make sure he is captured for posterity.

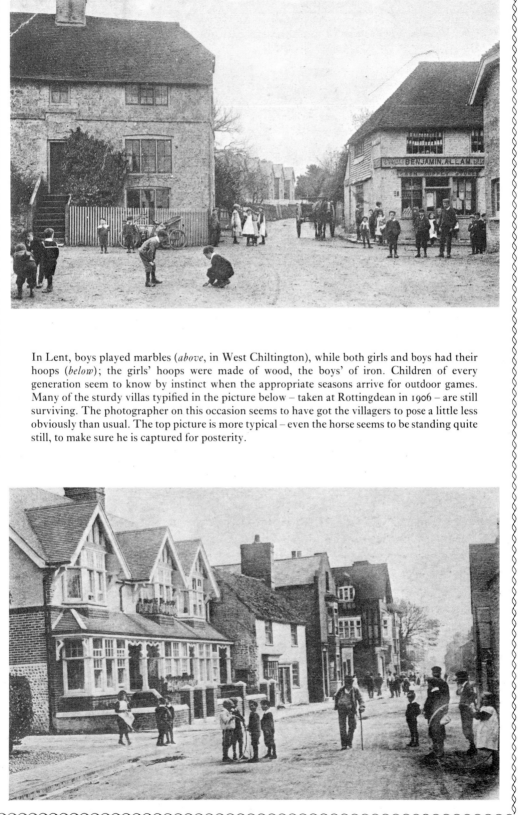

although recent years have seen attempts at revivals in other places. At Tinsley Green, outside the Greyhound pub, teams with names like Tinsley Green Tigers, Telcon Terribles, Johnson Jets, Cambridge Crackpots, Masked Marvels, Hirst Horribles, Teenage Twisters, Copthorne Cherrypickers and Copthorne Spitfires compete each year. Some of the original atmosphere has been lost with the influx of TV crews, foreign tourists and the like, and there is now an attempt to move the whole thing from its traditional home to the new Crawley Sports Centre.

The local story to account for this yearly game is of a village maiden for whose hand local players once competed. But this is almost certainly a modern fabrication. The game undoubtedly belongs to the widespread Sussex tradition of Lenten and Good Friday marble playing.

One of the most famous of the Tinsley Green players was George (Pop) Maynard, equally well known as a fine folk singer.

As a children's game, marbles was essentially for winter, and mainly for boys, although my mother remembered playing it each year in the streets of Horsham. This is how she described it as played by children eighty years ago: 'The marbles were played with a big ring enclosing a small ring, which contained the marbles contributed by each player. Each had a big marble to play with, called a "tolly", in order to get the marbles right out of the bigger ring. Any they got out, they had. They kept their marbles in a bag.' There were many other versions.

The girls had their own winter games – skipping, accompanied by many

Windmills were once a very familiar part of the Sussex landscape and each had its name. Most of the Sussex windmills disappeared long before people talked of conservation, although a few survive in varying stages of repair. 'Jill' (*above*), at Clayton, is still there, although she is showing increasing signs of her great age. Brother 'Jack' stands close by, on the Downs north of Brighton. 'Jill' was once moved across the Downs on wagons lashed together and drawn by a team of oxen. Cripplegate Mill (*below*), at Southwater, was burnt down on 25 May 1914. Made entirely of wood, it was almost totally destroyed by the time the fire engines got there. (*Top photo: Sussex Archaeological Society.*)

skipping rhymes, just as they are still, and hoops. Hoops were also popular with the boys, but where the girls' were of wood, the boys' were always of iron. My mother and my aunts looked on their hoops rather like cycles (which they couldn't afford) and took them with them whenever they went on an errand. The hoops carried them along the traffic-free streets in double-quick time and they hardly noticed the distance they had to travel.

And so to Easter Day, with few traditions to single it out in Sussex. One old, but rather cynical, belief was that on Easter Sunday you could see the sun dancing for joy if you got up early enough – except that the Devil always managed to put a hill in the way . . .

◇ ◇ ◇

Nowadays, folklorists are very interested in the ephemeral rhymes and taunts that were once heard constantly in our Sussex streets or playgrounds (the two were often synonymous); but there was a time when these were so commonplace that no one bothered to notice them. They were sometimes cruel, often funny, and usually to the point. Most of the examples which follow come from the recollections of my mother and older relatives and friends.

Many were parodies of well-known songs. For instance, to the tune of *Tramp, Tramp, Tramp*:

> *Don't I wish I was a Bobby,*
> *Dressed in other people's clothes,*
> *With a tummy full of fat*
> *And a coal-scuttle hat,*
> *And a pancake tied to my nose.*

And this one, to a well-known bugle tune:

> *Here comes the Boy's Brigade,*
> *All covered in marmalade,*
> *A twopenny-halfpenny pillbox,*
> *And half a yard of braid.*

Obviously, a uniform was always fair game:

> *The Royal Sussex is going today,*
> *Leaving the girls in the family way.*
> *Seven-and-six a week they'll pay,*
> *All for joining the army.*

Rude and crude they often were:

> *You're the Cock of the North, my boy,*
> *And I'm the Cock of the South.*

32

Above left: a fine tower mill at Barnham which is, happily, still there, although this picture was taken in 1905. The miller's cart and some of the mill stones can be seen. The mill is still owned by the Baker family. *Above right:* Lullington Church, famous as the smallest church in England, although this is really only the chancel of what was once a much larger building. *Below:* Preston church, Brighton, around 1900. Once part of a charming village, Preston has now been virtually swallowed up by its ever-expanding neighbour.

If you don't get out of the —— way,
I'll smack you round the mouth.
Cockadoodle, cockadoodle,
I'm the Cock of the South.

Tell tell tit, your tongue shall be split,
And all the dogs of Chailey Green
Shall have a little bit.

Minorities were also thought well worthy of attention:

The Lord said unto Moses,
All the Jews shall have long noses,
All except for Aaron,
And he shall have a squar'un.

Nebuchandessar, King of the Jews,
Sold his wife for a pair of shoes,
When the shoes began to wear,
Nebuchandessar began to swear.

There was little of today's religious tolerance seventy years ago, and what there was was pretty rough and ready. Roman Catholics were 'Catlicks' and C of E's 'Prodidogs'. But then, 'Sticks and stones may break my bones, but names will never hurt me.'

Just as well, as youthful humour has never been noted for its 'niceness'. A rhyme which went with a hand-game using a white (?) handkerchief was:

Dearly beloved Brethren,
Is it not a sin
To eat raw potatoes
And throw away the skins?
The skin feeds the pigs,
The pigs feed you,
Dearly beloved Brethren,
Is it not true?

Individuals sometimes featured in rhymes:

Old Foster drove the pigs to pound,
To buy his daughter a new silk gown.

(Foster was apparently once the landlord of the Royal Oak, at Wisborough Green.)

The next one has a transatlantic flavour, although it came from my mother:

Sam, Sam, dirty old man,

34

Oxen were once a familiar sight on many Sussex farms. They were liked for their ability to pull steadily. But George Townsend, of Lewes, told me, 'Horses for me every time! Oxen were very ignorant, not like horses, who seem to know what you say to them, once they get used to your voice.' There were both disadvantages and advantages to owning oxen. Shoeing them was a troublesome procedure – they had to be held down to make sure the smith wasn't injured by their horns. But when their working days were over, they could be fattened and sold for meat. No one seems to know for sure why it was that farmers stopped using them, which they did even before the advent of steam and petrol, turning universally to the horse. *(Top photo: Sussex Archaeological Society.)*

Oxen at Work in Sussex.

Washed his face in the frying pan,
Combed his hair with an engine wheel,
Died with a toothache in his heel.

Some rhymes were associated with, or remembered from, street traders:

Ladies with blue eyes,
Ladies with true eyes,
Ribbons and laces for sweet, pretty faces,
Oh, come to the market and buy!

Brandy balls as big as St Paul's,
Who will buy my brandy balls?

Hokey, Pokey, penny a lump,
Enough to make the Devil jump!

Young lambs to sell, white lambs to sell,
If I'd as much money as I could tell,
I wouldn't be crying young lambs to sell!

'Finders keepers' held true then as now, but sometimes the owner would be invited to claim his property:

Who's lost, and I found,
Picked it up upon the ground,
It isn't black and it isn't brown,
And it isn't worth half a crown.

The next has a plaintive air about it:

Teddy on the railway, picking up stones,
Along came an engine and broke Teddy's bones.
Oh! said Teddy, that's not fair,
Oh! said the engine, I don't care.

But they weren't despondent for long – there was always something to cheer about:

Cheer, boys, cheer, Mother's got a baby.
Cheer, boys, cheer, Mother's got a son.
Cheer, boys, cheer, Mother's bought a mangle.
Cheer, boys, cheer, she's filled it full of stones.
Cheer, boys, cheer, she makes me turn the handle.
Cheer, boys, cheer, it nearly breaks my bones.

And so back to crudity:

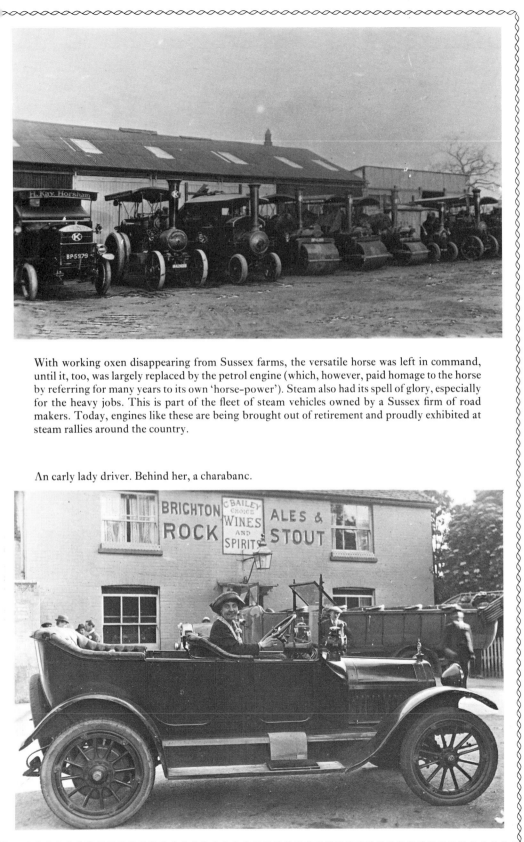

With working oxen disappearing from Sussex farms, the versatile horse was left in command, until it, too, was largely replaced by the petrol engine (which, however, paid homage to the horse by referring for many years to its own 'horse-power'). Steam also had its spell of glory, especially for the heavy jobs. This is part of the fleet of steam vehicles owned by a Sussex firm of road makers. Today, engines like these are being brought out of retirement and proudly exhibited at steam rallies around the country.

An early lady driver. Behind her, a charabanc.

Tiddly Winks the barber
Went to shave his father.
The razor slipped and cut his lip,
Tiddly Winks the barber.

I was born one day when me mother was out
And my father wasn't at home,
Hi Rickety Barlow,
Cock-a-doodle-do

Moses was a good man, of children he had seven.
He thought he'd hire a donkey cart and drive them all to heaven.
Strange to say, he lost his way: he thought he knew it well.
He overturned the donkey cart and landed them in hell.

Meat, fish and savoury dishes

Many of these old recipes were of the kind to provide good, solid food which would keep a man going during a long day working in the fields. Not for us Sussex folk the dainty and the delicately tempting. Wives knew that they had to feed their men with good, nourishing dishes, and as cheaply as possible. Hence the number of recipes featuring pastry and suet dough, many of them the sort of things which the men took into the fields with them for their midday meal, or 'bait'.

SUSSEX FRITTERS

$\frac{1}{2}$ *lb cold boiled potatoes*	*Breadcrumbs*
2 oz minced ham	*Pepper*
1 teaspoon chopped parsley	*Salt*
1 egg	

Mash the potatoes. Mix in the minced ham, parsley, pepper and salt, and the beaten yolk of the egg. Shape into small balls, egg and breadcrumb them and fry. Serve hot or cold.

Top left: a Sussex homestead at Balcombe, 1905. It may look attractive, but life for this old lady would have been anything but idyllic. *Top right:* the hardy men of the Hastings fishing fleet, April 1908. *Bottom left:* the Devil's Dyke, now as quiet as any place on the Downs, once boasted three railways, of which this is one. Traces of the track can still be seen. *Bottom right:* the brandy balls seller of Brighton – Dizzy was his name – was one of many such street salesmen of his day.

HASTINGS GURNET

The gurnet, or gurnard, is a rather ugly, spiny-finned fish, with an angular head and numerous small teeth.

Cut off the heads, wash well and dry. Dip in flour and pour melted dripping over them. Cut the skins and grill, turning them over twice. Serve hot with a little melted butter.

(From E. Manvel, of Broadbridge Heath.)

FRIED MACKEREL

Mackerel	*Onions*
Flour	*Mustard sauce*
Butter	

Clean the mackerel and cut off the heads. Wipe dry and roll in flour. Fry gently on both sides in a little butter. Serve with fried onions and mustard sauce.

GRILLED MACKEREL

Mackerel	*Lemon juice*
Parsley	*Seasoning*
Butter	

Split the mackerel and take out the backbone. Place on the grill pan, skin side up, and cook until heated through. Take out and spread the cut side with a liberal amount of parsley butter (finely chopped parsley pounded into butter, with lemon juice and seasoning). Put the fish back under the grill and cook slowly until the tops are brown. Spread more of the parsley butter on top and serve immediately.

OLD SUSSEX POTATO AND CHEESE CAKES

½ lb cooked potatoes	*1 egg*
2 oz flour	*Butter*
2 oz grated cheese	*Salt*

Wash the cooked potatoes with butter and salt. Add the flour, grated cheese and the egg, well beaten. Mix well together. Roll out and make into small round cakes. Bake in the oven or cook on the griddle.

(Published in *Sussex County Magazine*, vol. 10.)

CLAVERSHAM RISSOLES

These are rissoles made in the usual way, but with the addition of chopped celery, thyme, parsley, marjoram and breadcrumbs.

(From E. Manvel, of Broadbridge Heath.)

Above: the fishermen of Hastings (here persuaded by the photographer to drape themselves about their boat rather like maidens on a vase) are even today a community apart, with the same family names predominating through many generations. Although now members of a much smaller industry, these and the fishermen of other Sussex towns are proud of their links with the early history of the Sussex coast, which long predates its modern image as an endless row of holiday resorts. *Below:* the black net shops are a distinctive feature of the Hastings beach which fronts the old town. The traditional design, carefully preserved, is in the style first established in Elizabethan times. The shops are used for storing the fishermen's huge nets and tackle.

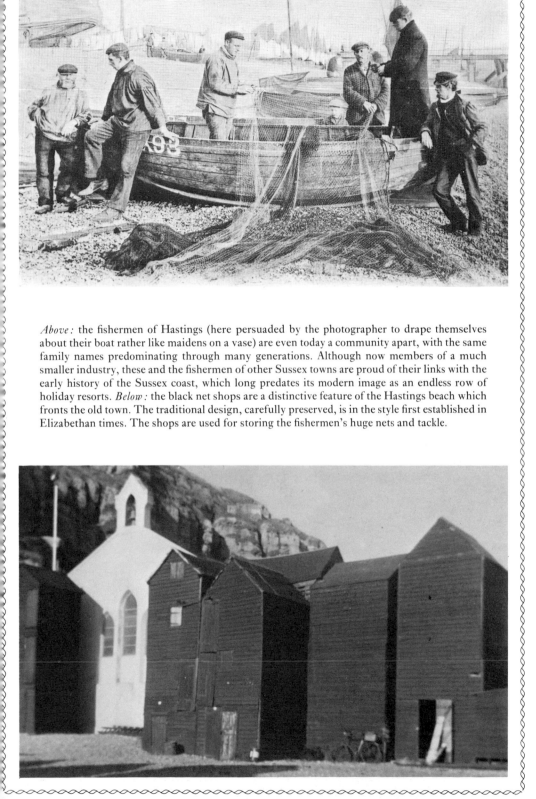

MARROW STEW

1 marrow	*Teaspoon Demerara sugar*
6 tomatoes	*Salt*
2 onions	*Pepper*
Lump of butter	*Bread and butter*

Peel and remove seeds from marrow and cut into small cubes. Skin tomatoes. Peel and cut onions. Place together in an enamel saucepan, with enough water to cover the bottom of the pan. Add butter, sugar, salt and pepper to taste. Stew slowly for $1\frac{1}{2}$–2 hours. Serve with toast or bread and butter.

SOUSED MACKEREL

4 small mackerel	*Mustard*
Salt	*Sugar*
Pepper	*Bay leaves*
Pickling spice	*Vinegar*

Clean the mackerel. Cut off the heads, wipe dry and lay them in a thick-bottomed saucepan. Sprinkle with salt, pepper and a big pinch of pickling spice. Add a little made mustard, a few lumps of sugar, one or two bay leaves, and just enough vinegar and water to cover – about two parts vinegar to one of water. Bring to the boil. Lower the heat and simmer for 15–20 minutes.

May Day and
Midsummer

MAY DAY no longer means what it once did in Sussex, although happy revivals of May ceremonies take place at several places, notably Chichester and Shoreham. As is often the case nowadays, these celebrations are in the capable hands of the local Morris Men or the local folk dance club. Of course, schools also celebrate May Day, but with Maypole plaiting dances, which are not really traditionally English.

The keeping of May Day in a special way is a very ancient custom, formerly observed by young adults. Later, as with many customs, children became its custodians.

Up to about 1900, it was common for 1 May to be called 'Garland Day' in Sussex. The chants were, 'Please remember the Garlands,' or, 'The first of May is Garland Day.'

In Petworth, the chant took the form of a rhyme:

> *The first of May is Garland Day,*
> *So please remember the Garland.*
> *We don't come here but once a year,*
> *So please remember the Garland.*

Quite obviously, this was just another way for children to cadge a few extra pennies, but the evidence is that, at best, it was a charming custom, encouraged by many grownups. Early on May Day, groups of children would collect their garlands of flowers and then go from door to door, soliciting contributions. Sometimes, considerable trouble would be taken over the flowers. One man told me he remembered a chair being decorated with flowers the day before, then let down into a well for the night, to keep the flowers fresh. On May Day itself, the chair became the May Queen's throne.

In 1771, it is recorded, a German prince staying at Brighton was visited by a group of little girls carrying garlands. And the custom sometimes spread over more than one day. On 2 May 1881, a Sussex school logbook carried the note, 'Several children absent carrying Garlands and flowers.'

By the start of the present century, the custom was becoming a little threadbare. In Horsham, children would go to a big house opposite the school in Clarence Road, carrying a bunch of flowers (or even weeds!) and there they would receive a halfpenny. The same children would return again and again, each time dressed a little differently. (This seems a rather depressing contrast to the practice of Mrs Tredcroft, of Manor House in the Causeway, Horsham, who used to have a special railed platform erected, from which she would receive her Garland visitors and hand out money.)

The flowers most often used for the Garlands were those which one would expect to find easily at that time of the year: cowslips, primroses and bluebells. Tied on the end of a long stick, rather like a multi-coloured mop, they must have made a pretty sight at the start of the day, though they would have wilted rather by the afternoon!

In Horsham, at the end of the last century, Mrs Smallwood, a milk seller, visited each of her customers on May Day with a trolley pulled by boys. The trolley carried a huge May Garland and a model cow: an enjoyable piece of public relations which Mrs Smallwood kept up until she was ninety-six.

May Day was also a special day for chimney sweeps, who would dress up in fancy costumes and carry evergreens round the town, accompanied by a fiddler. Different parties would vie with each other and there would be horseplay and generous drinking before the day was through.

◌   ◌   ◌

Towards the end of May, another, perhaps less attractive, custom was observed in Sussex. This was 'Pinching Day' or 'Pinch Bum Day', on 29 May. Also known as 'Oak Apple Day', it commemorated the birthday of Charles II and the day on which he returned from exile. Children who did not mark the day by wearing oak leaves were pinched or slashed with stinging nettles. One man, now a Sussex resident, told me that a similar custom was observed at his London school, but there it was considered sufficient to wear something green, although nobody knew why they were doing so.

Brighton fishermen, clinging once again to the old beliefs longer than landsmen, would take branches of oak to sea on 29 May.

One other May-time belief (which has some medical evidence to support it): to lose a corn, walk barefoot for the first three days of the month.

◌   ◌   ◌

Whitmonday was the day on which the old village clubs traditionally held their processions and feasts. Before the National Health Service, or any form of national insurance, had been instituted, Sussex villagers organised their own form of insurance against ill health or death, by means of 'clubs' or friendly societies. This type of organisation has a history going back several hundred years, but it proliferated in the nineteenth century, particularly in the South

Although not an English custom, the ribbon-plaiting dances around the Maypole have taken a firm hold in this country and most people think of this as the traditional English May Day ceremony, rather than our own, taller Maypole and the May Garlands, which have completely died out. This picture was taken at Battle Abbey's May carnival.

'May Revels', photographed in 1920 at Stanford Road School, Brighton. Schools were by this time beginning to take over the old customs. Of course, in doing so they were preventing their total extinction, yet it could also be said that formal performances of the kind illustrated lent an artificiality to what had originally been free-and-easy, unselfconscious celebrations.

and West of England. At the annual Whitmonday meeting, with its special ceremonies, members wore their best clothes – often smocks, sometimes with the addition of top hats, white gloves or coloured sashes – and carried banners, flags, staves, rods or, in Sussex, hazel wands. Mrs Nellie Perigoe, of Northiam, wrote to me in 1963: 'The Northiam Club ceased when National Insurance came in. On the annual club day, the men dressed in their "smocks" (one old gentleman called them "the emblem of purity"). They marched to church and then back, calling at a pub for bread and cheese, and on to the village green, where a meal was provided in a marquee erected on the grass near the Six Bells pub.'

CHARLES II in disguise in the Oak, sees his Persuers under him

Mrs Perigoe had lived in Northiam all her life and said her grandfather and great-grandfather had both taken part in the club-day processions.

Not all the Sussex clubs faded away in the face of national competition, it should be added. The Harting Old Club, on the Sussex-Hampshire border, was founded about 1800 and is still going strong. A few years ago, I was told by Mr Donald R. Noelle, the senior trustee, that the club had over £800 invested and that new members were still being enrolled. The subscription at that time was 35p per quarter, with a benefit payment of 75p a week during sickness. The funeral benefit was five pounds, with three pounds on the death of a member's wife. There was also a retirement pension.

The club at South Harting has been chronicled throughout its years of

Staplefield, May Day, 1921. The shepherds, wearing smocks and carrying crooks, have decorated their sheep with May Garlands – an unusual variation on an old custom.

'Club Day' at Iden, 27 May 1909. The clubs and friendly societies did sterling work supporting the old and the sick in the days before national insurance and other social welfare benefits. Few of them are still in existence.

existence by many writers. The three main items during the annual club day are the walk, the church service and the feast. The last is far from being the least important. On one occasion, the following amounts of food were provided for the hearty appetites of a hundred club members: three 15 lb gammons, 40 lb of veal, 14 lb topside, 40 lb of salt beef, two legs of pork, six yards of suet pudding and seventy-two gallons of beer. Folklorists will find in the ceremonies many items of interest. The peeled staves carried by the church members on their walk, for instance, are said to represent the staves the Canterbury Pilgrims carried as they passed by the village.

As I write this, I hear of the death of the Barns Green Friendly Society, which has a history going back 126 years. As with other clubs, the Barns Green society had an annual outing, assembling at the Queen's Head before setting off in procession, headed by a band, for a service at Itchingfield church – halting on the way at no fewer than three points for refreshment. Lunch was in a marquee, and one member described the day as 'a right binge'. Now, like most of the other Sussex clubs, this one has passed into history.

◦ ◦ ◦

SHEEP-SHEARING.

One of the most important periods in the village calendar was the sheep-shearing in JUNE. The job was usually undertaken by a gang, or 'company', with a captain and a lieutenant. The captain's cap was of the peaked variety, with gold braid; the lieutenant's was silver-braided. During the shearing, the farmer would say, 'Wool is scarce this year, boys! Shear 'em close, shear 'em close!' The captain would repeat this at appropriate times. Once the job had started, the only interruption was the shout of 'Tar boy!' when one of the sheep received a nick. The boy was there to dab the cut with tar to keep the flies away. It was not considered a good thing for a shearer to find it necessary to shout 'Tar boy!' too often. Although they were hard men and hard drinkers, they were good workers and proud of their art.

In spite of their special skills, the shearers could not work through the year, so they had to find other work, usually farm labouring. At the start of the sheep-shearing time, the gang would meet at the home of the captain for a feast called 'the White Ram'. There the whole campaign was planned with military

Sheep under Caburn: a picture which gives some idea of the size of the sheep population on the Sussex Downs just before the turn of the century.

Mr Stanford, shepherd, with dog and sheep, at Ringmer chalk pit around 1900. As the sheep grazed on the Downland turf, they swallowed many of the tiny white snails common to the region. It was these, it was said, which gave Southdown mutton its distinctive flavour.

precision. At the end of each day's work, they would eat supper at the farmhouse, smoke their pipes and sing songs. At the end of the season, earnings were split up at the captain's house. This was called 'shearing the Black Ram'. At one time, there were even county competitions – East Sussex against West Sussex, for instance.

23 June, Midsummer's Eve, was traditionally the Fairies' night. If you went into the fields this night and made a wish, it was certain to be granted. Fairies in Sussex were known as Farisees, or Pharisees. One man described them as 'little creatures rather bigger than a squirrel, and not quite as large as a fox'. Another said they were 'liddle folks not more than a foot high'. The fact that Pharisees are mentioned in the Bible was considered good evidence of their existence. Many Sussex place-names point to the firmly-held belief in fairies throughout the county: Faygate, Pookbourne, Pook Hole, Pook-Ryde, Pook Hale and Puck's Church Parlour, to mention just a few.

The Sussex fairies' colour was green and even today there is a belief among some folk that this is an unlucky colour to wear:

> *Those dressed in blue have lovers true.*
> *In green and white, forsaken quite.*

The fairy most often mentioned in Sussex was Dobbs, or Master Dobbs, known for his helpfulness with household tasks. If you did more work than was expected of you, you might be asked, 'Has Master Dobbs been helping you?' But, like most fairies, Dobbs was easily offended and withdrew his help if you were unwise enough to hurt his feelings.

Sussex folklore provides many stories about fairies, variants of most of which can be found in the folklore of other counties. Horses found exhausted in the morning were thought to have been ridden during the night by fairies, or by witches. (More probably the culprits were smugglers, who had a habit of borrowing horses without bothering to ask permission.)

One of the more attractive fairy stories from Sussex comes from Beeding, where two thieves once stole a pig, which they popped into a sack. When they stopped for a rest at the foot of Beeding Hill, they put the sack down with its opening over a hole in which lived a fairy. The little man decided to release the pig and take its place. As the two thieves climbed the hill, they heard a voice calling, 'Dick, Dick, where are you?' 'In a sack, pick-a-back, riding up Beeding Hill,' came the response from inside the sack. This story has all the hallmarks of a genuine fairy tale.

Chanctonbury Ring, on the South Downs, has been called the most magical place in Sussex. Fairies, the Devil and other supernatural beings are said to frequent the Ring and Midsummer Eve, that most magical of all days, is the time to watch for them – at midnight, of course. Even in modern times, people who have spent the night on the Ring have spoken of very strange sensations.

Sheep-washing somewhere in Sussex at the turn of the century. Note the contrast between the men in their working clothes and the mother (or nursemaid) with child, sitting prettily on the wall.

When the Sussex Downs really meant sheep. This is one of the famous dew ponds, at Falmer. The apparent mysteries of the dew ponds have caused controversy for years, but one thing is certain: without such ponds, the vast numbers of sheep which once inhabited the Downs would not have survived.

If it rains on St Swithin's Day, 15 JULY, it is said it will rain for forty days. That would mean a wet day for the annual Horn Fair at Ebernoe, which is held on or near 25 July, St James's Day. The origins of this ancient custom are unknown and, although a cricket match is now an important ingredient, the fair must go back further than the start of cricket in Sussex. Nowadays, there is a conventional fair, with stalls and sports, plus the cricket match and the roasting of a horned sheep. This is put on a hand-turned spit very early in the morning. The mutton provides the cricketers' lunch and the horns are given to the batsman scoring the most runs. The spit is kept at a local pub. At one time, it was a deer that was roasted and, earlier still, a wild ox. Like many customs, the Horn Fair has had its declines and revivals. Today, 3,000 visitors will turn up if St Swithin has been kind and it has even been televised. The Horn Fair song has been sung since 1951, following its rediscovery by Francis Collinson. Ralph Vaughan Williams also collected a version of the song at Kingsfold, in 1904.

There is another Horn Fair, at Charlton, in Kent, which is held on St Luke's Day, 18 October. An old saying goes, 'All is fair at Horn Fair', but this would seem to be more applicable to the Kent fair than our Sussex one, as at Charlton the day's festivities are said to be accompanied by considerable drinking and merrymaking: unlike Ebernoe, where everything goes off with great decorum.

There has always been a tradition of thunder on the day of Horn Fair. A thunderstorm during the day meant good crops and good luck. No storm and the crops and luck alike would be bad.

↶ ↷ ↶

Summer is the time for flower shows and at Worthing a companion told me how, seventy years ago, at the end of a local flower show, there was always dancing for the young people. After dark, they formed a large circle and played a game once very popular in Sussex, called 'kiss in the ring'. He said that many a young man met his future wife in this pleasant fashion.

I am sure there has always been dancing in Sussex, although few traditional dances have survived in the county. One of the exceptions is the 'Sussex Bonny Breast Knot', which is still danced to its very attractive tune. Folk dancing must have virtually died out in Sussex by the end of the nineteenth century, as it had in most of the South of England. It came back via the schools early in the twentieth century – and as a rather 'precious' activity among adults, with the taint of a schoolroom subject. In the past thirty years, however, along with folk song, it has undergone another revival and there is now probably more folk dancing going on in Sussex than at any time for the past hundred years. It is usually called barn dancing these days, and it often takes place in actual barns, many of these beautiful old buildings having been renovated for the purpose. But barn dances are also held in working barns, just as they must have been

Summer day trips, evening outings and (especially) mystery tours by motor charabanc were very popular once this form of transport had established itself. Kingsfold (*above*) was a popular stopping place. Note the pair of nigger minstrels on the left, playing to their 'captive' audience.

A complete fleet of motor vehicles owned by a Warnham family firm and photographed for an advertisement in 1929. Small businesses running buses, coaches and perhaps a lorry or two were viable concerns in those days, but gradually most of them have been absorbed by larger firms.

PHONE: HORSHAM 313.

J. MITCHELL,
WARNHAM STATION,
Nr. HORSHAM, SUSSEX.

PHONE: HORSHAM 313.

14 Seater   and   20 Seater Cars   1 Ton Lorries
For Hire.

centuries ago, and the sounds of the cattle sometimes mingle with the dance music. Although we cannot claim many surviving traditional dances, new dances in the old style are being composed, with Sussex names like 'Chichester Cross', 'Coolham Waltz' and 'Chanctonbury Ring'.

◇ ◇ ◇

The warm month of AUGUST is also the beginning of the end of summer – as the old saying goes, 'In August, summer spells farewell.' 24 August is St Bartholemew's Day, and another saying has it that 'St Bartholemew brings the cold dew.'

Earlier in the month, another charming custom used to be observed in the Brighton streets. This was on 5 August, when children built grottoes on the pavements, using oyster shells. The cry was, 'Penny for the grotto!' Like so many customs, it had faded away by the start of this century.

◇ ◇ ◇

No doubt anyone who married in the summer hoped for sunny weather. But there were also other things to worry about – for instance:

> *Change your name, but not your letter,*
> *Change for the worse and not for the better.*

The colour of the bride's dress was important:

> *Married in black, you wish yourself back.*
> *Married in blue, love will be true.*
> *Married in brown, you'll live in the town.*
> *Married in yellow, ashamed of the fellow.*
> *Married in green, not fit to be seen.*
> *Married in pink, you'll live at the sink.*
> *Married in red, you'll wish you were dead.*
> *Married in purple, you'll look simply awful.*
> *Married in grey, you'll live right away.*
> *Married in mauve, you'll look like a toad.*
> *Married in white, you'll look just right.*

If you missed out on marriage, there was a rhyme for you:

> *Ah me, my poor heart's sad,*
> *The young man's married I ought to have had.*
> *Or if he's not married, he's bespoke.*
> *And that's the reason my heart's broke.*

But there was always the thought:

> *Needles and pins, needles and pins,*

Above: 'Uncle Charlie's Children's Corner', on the Green at Littlehampton in 1938. A generation of children grew up delighting in Charlie. Indeed, Littlehampton became known as the resort which catered particularly for children. *Below:* another view of Littlehampton, this time showing the tiny pier, from which you could always hope to see a ship like this one. I can myself recall the windmill on the right, which was pulled down fifty years ago to make way for an amusement park. I remember the unique feel of the outside wall in the hot sunshine. My grandfather, who had once been a miller, helped to demolish it and one of the timbers he saved is still in use as a clothes post, bearing the date '31 July 1868'.

When you get married, your trouble begins.

Shoes gave your secret away:

> *Wear at the toe, you spend as you go,*
> *Wear at the heel, you spend a great deal.*

Dreams were always very important:

> *A Friday's dream on a Saturday told*
> *Is sure to come true if it's ever so old.*

Even cutting nails has its own rhyme:

> *Monday for health,*
> *Tuesday for wealth,*
> *Wednesday the best day of all,*
> *Thursday for crosses,*
> *Friday for losses,*
> *And Saturday no luck at all.*
> *But a child whose nails on a Sunday are shorn*
> *Will live to wish he'd never been born.*

Another belief was that, if you cut your nails on a Sunday, the Devil would chase you all week. Of course, days of the week were even more important when it came to being born. As in other counties, it was said that:

> *Monday's child is fair of face,*
> *Tuesday's child is full of grace,*
> *Wednesday's child is full of woe,*
> *Thursday's child has far to go,*
> *Friday's child is loving and giving,*
> *Saturday's child works hard for a living,*
> *But a child that is on the Sabbath born*
> *Is bonny and blithe and full of song.*

In fact, it was very satisfactory to be born on a Sunday, as this also ensured security from drowning and hanging.

Those born at three, six, nine or twelve o'clock were supposed to possess the faculty of seeing much that is hidden from others.

Even Christian baptism had its associated superstitions. It was thought unlucky for the child not to cry while being baptised. The Holy Water used should not be wiped off the child's head. It was unlucky to divulge the child's name before baptism.

There were so many superstitions in years past that it is surprising that people who believed them ever had the courage to get through each day! For

56

The pleasures of the seaside were heightened by the rarity of the experience for many people. These paddlers at Bognor seem to be having a good time in spite of their cumbersome attire.

This family of seaside trippers at Bexhill, complete with Grandad and Grandma, seem a little embarrassed at facing the photographer. The year is 1914 and soon the young men in the picture will be in khaki on the other side of the Channel.

instance, itching had a deep significance: Itch on the feet? Tread on fresh ground. Itch on the elbow? A fresh bedmate. Itch on the hand? Money to come. Itch on the nose? A stranger coming, a kiss, or a curse. Tingling in the right ear? Someone speaking well of you. Tingling in the left ear? Someone speaking ill of you.

Before central heating and other modern types of heating, the open fire was an important point in the house – and an important source of signs. If a fire burned hollow in the middle, this meant a parting; if it burned well when first lit, your sweetheart or husband was good-tempered; if it wouldn't burn, then he (or she) was bad-tempered; if a square-shaped coal fell out of the fire, this meant a present; if a coffin-shaped coal fell out of the fire, this meant a death; to dream of a fire meant urgent news; and if the kettle on the fire spat, it meant welcome news.

Similar superstitions included: if a teapot lid was accidentally left off, this meant a stranger was coming to the house (also indicated by the dropping of a knife); a pair of shoes on the table meant a row was imminent; picking up a dropped umbrella meant a surprise in store.

Another indicator of a visitor was a tea-leaf floating on your cup of tea. This was referred to as a 'stranger', a large leaf suggesting a man and a small one a woman. One of my mother's talents, which she learned from my grandmother, was 'telling the tea-leaves'. Almost everyone liked to have their fortune told from the cup, although nobody would admit to believing in it. My mother didn't enjoy doing it very much and would never tell anyone what the signs and shapes were that she was looking at.

Many things were considered unlucky: seeing a Death's Head moth; opening an umbrella indoors; picking up your own glove; seeing a new moon through glass; having a picture fall without apparent cause; meeting someone with a cast in their eye; gathering cherry blossom; bringing hawthorn into the house; turning your stockings after you have put them on inside-out; meeting a cross-eyed person; seeing a large number of ladybirds; spilling salt (if you did, you had to throw it over your left shoulder, saying, 'I don't care.'); having a bird fly into the house; and seeing a magpie over your left shoulder.

There were far fewer things connected with good luck: seeing a brown-and-white Dalmation dog; finding and taking indoors a piece of coal; putting a goat in with sheep; picking up a horse shoe and keeping it; living in a house with laurel bushes round it (the laurel being the luckiest of all trees); and picking up a pin.

That last one even had its own rhyme:

> *See a pin and pick it up,*
> *All the day will bring good luck.*
> *But see a pin and pass it by,*

Marine Palace Pier, Brighton. "Hello, Boys,
I am coming"

One of Brighton's famous bathing-huts on wheels. You climbed down from the hut straight into the water, hence the size of the wheels. Sometimes the help of a bathing attendant was necessary.

The seafront at Bognor, at a time when the town was undecided about whether to aim at the popular image of a Brighton or the more sedate style of an Eastbourne, a dilemma which some feel Bognor never resolved.

Sorrow will greet you by and by.

You should always make a wish
 – when you see a piebald pony
 – when you eat the first fruit of the season.
And, lastly, some superstitions about sneezing:

One for a wish,
Two for a kiss,
Three for a letter,
Four for something better.

Almost all these beliefs came from my mother and were taken seriously in her family when she was young. Without the present-day distractions of modern entertainment, it was probably necessary to relieve the monotonous life that most people led by recourse to these and many other superstitions and charms.

Pies

An apple pie without the cheese
Is like a kiss without the squeeze.

So runs an old Sussex rhyme, although I have been unable to trace any particular recipe for a Sussex apple pie, other than that it should presumably be made with the addition of cheese rather than anything as 'cissy' as cream or custard.

PUMPKIN PIE

This is the dish my mother used to make when she particularly wanted to please my father. Some recipes call for pumpkin rather than marrow, but I give it as I remember my mother making it.

$\frac{1}{2}$ *lb marrow (weighed when chopped)*	$\frac{1}{4}$ *lb sultanas*
6 oz chopped apples	*Teaspoon ground ginger*
6 tablespoons sugar	*Little nutmeg*

Mix the ingredients together with a little water until they are all soft. Line a large plate with short pastry and spread the mixture over. Put on a top crust and bake until brown. Before serving, lift the lid and pour in three or four tablespoons of rich cream, if desired.

King's Road. *Dear Ettie I shal* Brighton.
Return about 30th 31th January S. P

This photograph of Brighton seafront, taken around 1910, has an Impressionistic flavour to it: the fine composition provides a picture full of fascinating detail. The handwriting, for all its haste (it was probably written at the post office counter) has a character impossible to convey in today's ubiquitous ballpoint.

An excellent view of the Kursaal at Bognor in 1915. The word 'kursaal', literally translated from the German, means 'cure saloon', but the early kursaals were gambling halls, where nothing was cured but wealth. They became more general amusement halls later. The Bognor Kursaal was eventually re-named the Theatre Royal.

HERB PIE

2 handfuls parsley	Flour
1 handful spinach	2 eggs
2 lettuces	1 pint cream
Mustard and cress	½ pint milk
Few leaves of burridge	White beet leaves

Wash the herbs, then boil them a little, drain, press out the water and cut them small. Mix and lay them in a dish sprinkled with salt. Mix a batter with flour, 2 well beaten eggs, a pint of cream and half a pint of milk and pour it on to the herbs. Cover with a good crust and bake.

(Published in *The Mistress of Stanton's Farm*, Marcus Woodward, 1938.)

TEN-TO-ONE PIE

This gets its name from the supposition that it contains ten pieces of potato to one of meat.

Pastry dough	Pickled pork
Potatoes	Pepper
Onions	Salt

Line a plate with the pastry. Fill with a layer of thinly-sliced raw potatoes, a layer of sliced onion and a layer of pickled pork. Add pepper and salt. Then add more potatoes and onions. Cover with pastry and bake for an hour and a half.

(Published in *Sussex County Magazine*, vol. 10.)

TOMATO PIE

4 oz shortcrust pastry	1 oz dripping or butter
1 shallot or onion	1 lb fresh tomatoes
4 oz breadcrumbs	2 oz grated cheese

Line a pie dish with thinly rolled-out pastry. Mix half the breadcrumbs and cheese in with the pulped tomatoes. Place in the pie dish with thinly-sliced shallot or onion. Season. Put the rest of the cheese and breadcrumbs on top of the mixture. Dot the top with dripping or butter and bake for 30 minutes in a moderately hot oven.

(From E. Tucker, of Brighton.)

VEGETABLE PIE

2 medium-sized carrots	Chopped parsley
1 large turnip	½ pint white sauce
1 small swede	2 tablespoons rice
1 onion	Small tin baked beans

The famous Long Man of Wilmington, cut into the side of a hill, watches over a team of oxen returning from the fields. Opinions differ about the origin and age of the giant, but there is widely held to be something primitively pagan in his bold outline.

Amberley church and castle. The 'castle' is actually only a fortified manor house. One of the many tunnel stories which abound in Sussex concerns a secret passage supposed to run from Arundel castle to Amberley.

Prepare vegetables. Slice onion and fry in fat left over from bacon. Cube carrots, swede and turnip and cook in salted water until tender. Steam rice over the pan. Mix vegetables, rice and beans. Place in pie dish. Add enough white sauce and parsley to bind. Cover with shortcrust and bake for 30 minutes.

(From E. Tucker, of Brighton.)

SUSSEX MOCK PORK PIE

Short pastry $\frac{1}{2}$ *teaspoon mixed herbs*
Bacon, 2–3 oz per person   *Pepper*
Eggs, 1 per person   *Salt*

Line shallow pie dish with pastry, arrange bacon pieces over and dust with pinch or more of mixed herbs. Break eggs carefully, to keep yolks intact, and pour over filling. Add seasoning. Cover with more pastry and bake in good oven for 1 hour. Eat hot or cold.

(From Mrs K. Earp, of Brighton. Originally printed in *Good Things in England*, ed. Florence White, Jonathan Cape, 1933: now available in paperback, published by Futura Books. Reprinted by permission.)

APPLE TURNOVER

8 oz self-raising flour   *2 oz butter*
4 oz margarine   *3 oz brown sugar*
Milk   *Nutmeg to taste*
2 large cooking apples

Make pastry with the flour, margarine and milk. Line a deep, greased plate with pastry and cover with apples, peeled and cut very small. Do not add any water. Put on a pastry lid and cook for $\frac{1}{2}$–$\frac{3}{4}$ hour at gas mark 6. When golden brown, remove from oven, cut off lid and mash apples, adding butter, brown sugar and nutmeg. Replace lid and press into mixture. Put back into oven for 10 minutes. Serve with custard or cream.

(From Mrs L. Puttock, of Roffey. It was one of her grandmother's recipes over seventy years ago.)

SOUTH-DOWN
SHEEP HOOK.

4

Harvest Homes and Halloween

HARVEST SUPPERS of the past were undoubtedly a good excuse for drinking, perhaps rather more well than wisely. But to the Sussex countryman of the past, drinking was part of normal daily life, anyway. He drank home-made beer or cider in the fields, the locally brewed variety in the pub and home-made wine at home. It was both a pleasure and an important part of his diet. The beer drunk in the fields was perhaps only half as strong as that made for consumption at other times but still as strong as that sold in pubs. Almost all the farms made cider, for the hands to drink and to offer to visitors. (A 'mug of cider' was often more than a pint.)

It seems strange that Sussex has never been considered cider country. George Attrill, of Fittleworth, told me how he and another man were employed annually to make the cider at one farm. It took them a week to make several hundred gallons. (It was stored in barrels with taps and one huge tank big enough to get inside to clean it out.) In spite of these quantities, it was all gone by the next year's cider-making time, and none was sold. It was much stronger than most of today's cider and very potent if you were not used to it. Special apples were used – ordinary ones would not do. They were very juicy, but like a piece of woollen rag to bite when raw. After the first making, water and extra sugar were added to the pulp to make a further, inferior batch. The apples used were not prepared in any way, but went into the press just as they had been picked, mud and all.

As can be understood, there was a certain amount of drinking to excess in years past, often as an indirect result of the hardness of the countryman's life. The 'good old days' were not all that good for many, and drink was sometimes the working man's only release from pain, worry or the sheer sordidness of the life he was forced to lead. The village pub was a social necessity. Despite the evils of over-drinking, much good also came out of it: the village clubs and friendly societies, for instance. But, of course, this was strictly a man's world, without the softening influence of wives or sweethearts, so there were always those who carried a good thing too far.

If any excuse for drinking were needed, then the toasts which most men knew by heart provided it. Here are a few of them:

> Here's luck to the man with the ragged coat,
> He's got no wife to mend it,
> Bad luck to the man with plenty of money,
> Who ain't got the belly to spend it.

The squeamish may prefer to skip the next one:

> Here's to Father Christmas, the King of the Jews,
> But not to the man that bad beer brews.
> He adds too much water and spoils good malt,
> May the Devil pick his eyes out and fill the holes with salt.

And some shorter ones:

> Here's to the bee that stung Adam
> And set the whole world a-jogging.

> Here's a health to the Queen Victoria,
> And may we always have her likeness in our pockets.

> May the soldier who loses one eye in the service of his country
> Never see distress with the other.

> Here's to the flea that jumped over me
> And bit my brother.

> T for tobacco and B for beer,
> The Devil take those that won't come here.

> May we never want a friend
> Or a pint to give him.

> Here's to the man who drinks enough to sink a barge
> And drinks enough to float it again.

> May the smuggler's heart be free from the pirate's spirit.

> May the bloom on the face never extend to the nose.

> Here's to the Irishman who spokeshaved his belly
> To make his trousers fit.

Irishmen were fair game for pub wit, even in those days. As for women, although pubs were no place for them, they were still in men's minds:

> Here's to man, God's first thought.
> Here's to woman, God's second thought.
> As second thoughts are best, here's to women.

Haymaking in Sussex in 1908 (*above*) and on 18 June 1905 (*below*), an unusually precise picture reference, though the farm concerned is not known. Haymaking was once something in which everybody – men, women and children – joined. Indeed, children were once such essential help in the fields during the busy seasons that village schoolteachers just had to resign themselves to losing most of their classes for a while. Haymaking usually came around the end of June, though the weather was always liable to change the farmer's best-laid plans.

Here's to the man who kisses his wife
And kisses his wife alone,
For there's many a man kissing other men's wives,
When he ought to be kissing his own.

And my favourite of all:

More pork and less parsons!

Some of the best Sussex songs are about drinking. George Attrill sang me his version of *John Barleycorn* in 1958. Not as well known as the usual *John Barleycorn*, but a rollicking good song.[1] Then there is the famed Copper Family song, *Good Ale*, from Rottingdean.[2] Michael Blann, one of our Sussex shepherds, wrote his song, *A Drop of Good Beer*, in his notebook, now preserved in Worthing Museum. And last but by no means least, there is the now often sung *Sussex Toast*,[3] popularised in the folk clubs by George Belton, from Madehurst, now living in retirement near Chichester. After drinking in turn to eight of his friends, George ends up with:

I have drunk nine, and I will drink ten.
Now I think it's my turn to drink again.

Most people take the slightly uncomplimentary remarks in the song (*There sits one who's in a very good fix* or *There sits one who will drink double his weight*) in good part, but one night in a pub a stranger offered to fight George over one of the verses. Happily, all was settled over another drink.

Strangely enough, although this is now considered a Sussex song, it probably did not originate in our county. George learned it, along with most of his songs, from his father and other older members of his family, and he originally came from Surrey. But as there are really no such things as county folk songs, only versions, this does not alter our claim to the song as it is sung today.

[1] Recorded by Dave and Toni Arthur on Topic 12T 190
[2] Recorded by Bob and Ron Copper on EFDSS LP1002
[3] Recorded by George Belton on EFDSS LP1008

Top left: the Farmer's Boy with his team of oxen on the Downs near Lewes and his goad (a long stick of hazel wood) with which to control them. *Top right:* the author's grandfather on his wife's side, Thomas Godsmark, of Burgess Hill. Family documents described him variously as a thatcher or a hay-cutter. Evidently, there was sometimes too little thatching to keep him occupied throughout the year – unlike today, when thatchers have waiting lists of clients needing their rare skills. *Below:* Mr Hollingdale with a loaded cart at Alciston, around 1900.

The following chant, given me by a staunch teetotaller, dates back to 1887:

> *We'll all get drunk and have a good spree,*
> *It's only once in fifty years – the Queen's jubilee.*

Perhaps even teetotallers celebrated on such occasions! Locally brewed ale always had its champions – for instance:

> *He who buys land buys stones,*
> *He who buys fish buys bones,*
> *He who buys eggs buys many shells,*
> *But he who buys good ale buys nothing else!*

But Sussex pubs sell other things besides ale these days. Here is a rhyme from a relatively modern sign on the Murrell Arms, at Barnham:

> *Mervyn Cutten liveth here,*
> *Sells brandy, whiskey, Geneva rum, snuff, baccy and beer.*
> *I've made a little wider sign,*
> *To let you know I sell good wine.*

Other Sussex pubs yield interesting drinking rhymes. From the Elephant and Castle, at West Chiltington, comes:

> *The wonderful love of a beautiful maid,*
> *And the love of a staunch true man,*
> *And the love of a baby unafraid,*
> *Have existed since life began.*
> *But the greatest love, the love of love,*
> *Even greater than that of a mother,*
> *Is the tender, passionate, infinite love*
> *Of one drunken sot for another!*

And from the White Horse, near Pulborough, a rhyme also known elsewhere:

> *Pure water is the best of gifts*
> *That man to man can bring.*
> *But who am I that I should have*
> *The best of everything?*
> *Let princes revel at the pumps*
> *And peers at the pond make free.*
> *But whiskey, wine and even beer*
> *Is good enough for me!*

Not all songs and rhymes were about the pleasures of drink. This temperance monologue came to me from Mr E. King, of West Grinstead, who

Sussex women with sacks of – what? Are they potatoes? sprouts? Can anyone offer a better suggestion? The photograph was too interesting to omit.

Schoolboys from a Sussex school around 1910, with their own crops. The headmaster looks on benignly, wearing his fashionable boater and the almost obligatory watch and chain. The author's father holds the Sussex trug basket on the left. When he left the school, he took with him a pocket watch bearing the inscription, 'Never absent, never late'.

learned it from his mother in 1890. It is called *Carter's Pints*, carters being the men who handled the horses on the farm. They were a cut above the rest of the farmhands. In many liquor shop windows of the period could be seen a notice stating, 'Carter's Pints from 6.00 a.m. to 6.00 p.m.' The words of the poem are typical of the temperance verse of the time:

> *I'm only an old-fashioned labouring man,*
> *More used to a plough than a pen,*
> *And still in good trim for a fair spell of work,*
> *Though close upon three score and ten.*
> *But though I be what folk would describe*
> *As an ignorant short of a chap,*
> *I've managed to learn that the public house bar*
> *Is a dangerous sort of a trap.*

> *And when I see notices stuck all about*
> *To draw working men in to drink,*
> *I feel I must try in my own humble way*
> *To let people know what I think.*
> *They've traps of all kinds for the thoughtless and weak,*
> *Poor folks who have nothing to spare,*
> *And threeha'pence a pint from six until six,*
> *Is the Carter's particular share.*

There are three more verses in similar killjoy vein, culminating in:

> *I'm not used to writing and things such as that,*
> *A fact that can easily be seen.*
> *But though I've a bungling fist for a pen,*
> *I think I've said straight wat I mean.*
> *But to make it more plain, let me say it again,*
> *To put working men on their guard:*
> *For it's time that they knew the false from the true,*
> *Then they need not work quite so hard.*

In a lighter vein, the following was sung to the tune of *We Won't Go Home Till Morning*:

> *We're all teetotallers here,*
> *We don't want any more beer.*
> *Shut up your public houses,*
> *Shut up your public houses,*
> *Shut up your public houses,*
> *We're all teetotallers here.*

Most advocates of temperance took the cause very seriously. The following

Not all hops were grown in Kent. Across the border, in East Sussex, hop-picking was just as important an annual event. Local hop pickers were strongly augmented by armies of casual workers from outside the district – particularly from London's East End. For these people, it was an annual holiday with pay and their only chance of sampling the delights of country life.

The familiar outlines of oast houses may still be seen in Kent and Sussex, although many of them have now been converted into private homes.

appeared in a Sussex newspaper in 1865, under the heading, 'A Word of Advice to the Poor Cottager':

> ... One thing especially they should guard against, and that is the beerhouse. No man is in so poor a condition that he can rise in some way, if he be not afflicted with physical infirmity. Therefore we say to the poor man and his wife – and the happiness of the home rests with the wife – strive to do your best for yourself ...

But the following is probably the most sweeping and outspoken condemnation of over-indulgence that you could find in Sussex. It appears on a wall in Kirdford, the message (it is said) having been slipped under the vicarage door during the incumbency of a Reverend Cole in the nineteenth century. Did the writer think that he needed the injunction?

> DEGRADATION OF DRUNKENNESS
>
> There is no sin which doth more deface God's image than drunkenness. It disguiseth a person and doth even unman him. Drunkenness makes him hath the throat of a fish, the belly of a swine and the head of an ass. Drunkenness is the shame of nature, the extinguisher of reason, the shipwreck of chastity and the murderer of conscience. Drunkenness is hurtful to the body, the cup kills more than the cannon, it causes dropsies, catarrhs, apoplexies. It fills the eye with fire, and the legs with water and turns the body into an hospital.

This is apparently the second such inscription to be inserted in the wall, so it must be looked upon as a valuable adjunct to the village.

No wonder feelings on drink ran high in the past, when we consider some of the effects detailed on that plaque. But, as the toast says, 'There are several good reasons for drinking,' and in the past they were not hard to find.

⋄ ⋄ ⋄

OCTOBER was the month when summer was finally forgotten. On 10 October, the Devil was supposed to spit on the blackberry bushes, and you should not gather the fruit after that date. Indeed, about this time the remaining blackberries are no longer worth the effort of picking.

25 October is St Crispin's Day, which is the shoemaker's patronal feast. Henry Burstow, of Horsham, said that they all got drunk in his honour. Anyone who had disgraced himself was held up to ridicule on this day, by means of an effigy hung outside the local pub. It was left there to be burnt on 5 November.

A custom known as Crispin's Crispian was annually celebrated at Slaugham. Boys used to run up and down the green, swinging burning heath brooms round and round and rolling a tar barrel down a steep hill. This was said to commemorate the Battle of Agincourt. A writer in 1922 noted that the custom had by then fallen into disuse.

⋄ ⋄ ⋄

My great-grandmother called Halloween (31 October) 'a night fit for neither

Top left: these hop-pickers are from Coolham, in West Sussex, not normally thought of as hop country. The large brimmed hats would have kept off the sun, but the long skirts must have posed problems. *Top right:* the Cockney hop-pickers were accommodated in the crudest of living quarters and disliked by local shopkeepers for their unfamiliar speech and rough manners. Consequently, services for them were either non-existent or makeshift, as in this picture, taken at Northiam in 1911. *Below:* a Sussex trug basket from Herstmonceaux. Anyone who has ever used one for gardening will never want to be without it.

God nor man'. My mother was told as a young girl that this was the night when all the unsettled souls were abroad. Certainly it was always looked upon as a very creepy and magical night and children in years past anticipated with a kind of enjoyable dread the many superstitions that surrounded it. If a young lady were to eat an apple and look in her mirror at midnight, she would see her future husband gazing at her over her shoulder. Everyone, animal and human, must turn over at midnight while asleep on this night, or they would not wake up alive.

◇ ◇ ◇

I grew up with dialect words and phrases used as a matter of course by my mother and my aunts. I didn't know they were dialect, as to begin with they were part of my normal stock of words, and later on they became family words, which you didn't use outside the house if you wanted to be understood and not laughed at.

When I was older, I came across *A Dictionary of the Sussex Dialect*, by the Reverend W. D. Parish, originally published in Lewes in 1875, and I was surprised and delighted to find many of my mother's words mentioned. Yet quite a number of her expressions did not appear, either because Parish had not come across them or, perhaps, because he had considered them mere slang rather than true dialect. Here is a brief list of some of the dialect and obsolete slang words used by my mother and other older members of the family:

Ackle – how a thing works correctly

Awk – a big, ungainly person

Bum-freezer – a short coat

Broom-dasher – an untidy person. (Parish merely gives the earlier meaning of 'a dealer of brooms'.)

Church-yarder – a very bad cough

Clung – half-dry washing

Dabtoe – a person who is a nuisance

Dander – temper

Delser – a small, neat thing

Dinlow – slow-witted

Disbelieving Jew – someone who is difficult to convince

Dossle – an article

Faggot (or *old faggot*) – an annoying person

Fat Jack – an annoying or slow-witted person

Fur my heel – annoy me

Furs Bush – the tune the cat sings when she is purring

Grizzle-guts – a grumbler

Hard tack – poor food

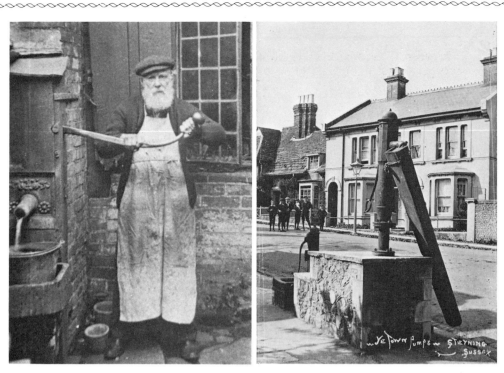

Top left: water, like so much else, is taken for granted nowadays, yet less than a century ago living in the country meant – unless you were fairly well off – pumping or hauling all your water requirements. This is Mr Voice, of Horsham, in 1905. *Top right:* street pumps in Steyning. The boys were obviously intrigued by the photographer. *Below:* the first job in the morning – drawing the water. If you were lucky, you had your own pump; if not, you went to the nearest one you could find, like these two. The original caption was 'Fur better or fur wurz'. 'Fur wurz' at this time of the day, one would think.

Hobbly-guts – a bus
Ibidioy – a lout
Ichen (or *ichell*) – as thick as
Jackdaws' parliament – a noisy gathering
Jawmedead – someone who talks a lot
Jollop (or *jipper*) – gravy
Lear – an empty feeling in the pit of the stomach. (Parish is less explicit,
    giving 'thin, hungry, faint'.)
Licker – a surprising thing
Longanner – a tall person
Lord Tom Noddy – someone who thinks himself important
Malook – daft or mad
Mermaid's purses – egg cases of the dogfish
Old apple woman – someone who fusses
Pig-sticker – a large knife
Pinch-plumb – a mean person
Purling – looking
Ragtush – an untidy person
Raw throat – a sore throat
Rubbishy-buster – an untidy person
Slew-ways – sideways
Soon – daft or slow-whitted
Spruse – to deceive
Spruser – someone who deceives
Struttik (*Not a* –) – not anything
Sussex lawyers – brambles
Sussex swedes (or *swede-gnawers*) – country people
Sweal – to scour clothes
Tibster – small man
Water bewitched – weak tea
Wounded beanstick – tall, thin person

Equally interesting are the phrases and sayings. Something done badly was 'done with a hot needle and a burning thread'. To do the impossible was to 'jump up and hang by nothing'. A very indolent person was said to be 'as lazy as spit water'. Someone very dishonest was 'as big a liar as Old Tom Pepper, and *he* was thrown out of Hell for lying.' To look surprised was to look 'nineways for Sunday'. To be very poor was to not have 'a faggot above a load'. To be in great trouble was to have 'the biggest land and the worst reap'. To take a lot of trouble for nothing was to 'strain at a gnat and swallow a sawmill'. Something without any curl was 'as straight as a yard of pump water'. A very evil person would 'say anything but their prayers, and them they'd whistle (or say

The beginning of another school year in Hickstead (*above*) and in Kirdford (*below*), in the days when even seven-year-olds were called scholars and the girls, and sometimes the boys, wore white pinafores to school. School buildings were usually purpose-built, often with their own small bell steeples. School life was spartan by today's standards. Children might walk several miles through every kind of weather to get to school and back. If they arrived with wet clothes and feet, they found little consolation: perhaps their wet coats could steam on the fireguard round the school stove, but shoes had to be kept on, as indoor shoes at school were unknown.

backwards).' An empty stomach after sickness was consoled with the thought that 'an empty house is better than a bad tenant.' In fact, there seemed to be a saying to meet every possible situation – or, as my aunt would say, 'a plaster for every wound'.

Rhymes were used to help in remembering facts or to point morals, or just for amusement:

> *Man to the mow,*
> *Boy to the sow,*
> *And maid to the cow.*

(No Women's Lib in those days!)

Those who don't shut doors in Sussex are said to 'come from Yapton'. Several origins have been suggested for this saying. One is that a Yapton farmer had a calf in a field. It put its head through the gate to eat a tasty bit of grass and got stuck. To free it, the farmer had to cut its head off; ever afterwards, he decreed that his gates should be left open.

One lady told me that when her nephew (who actually lived at Yapton) left a door open at a school he attended some way from home, a teacher said, 'You must come from Yapton!' The boy, much surprised, said, 'That's right – but how did you know?'

Sussex has always been noted for fictional place-names. As a boy, I always wondered why older people talked about Rusper Docks yet laughed when I asked to be taken to see the ships there. Then there are the Faygate (and Patcham) treacle mines. After one of my talks, someone asked me, tongue-in-cheek, if I had heard of the Colgate toothpaste mines. And there are shrimp boats at Didling Harbour and winkle barges at Pallingham Quay. I suspect there are others in more local circulation.

Lastly, here are a Sussex shepherd's words for counting his sheep:

One-erum,	*Shatherum,*
Two-erum,	*Wine-berry,*
Cockerum,	*Wagtail,*
Shu-erum,	*Tarrydiddle,*
Shitherum,	*Den.*

As the sheep were counted in pairs, 'den' stood for a score.

———

Traditional Sussex dishes

Some of our Sussex dishes seem to belong particularly to our own county – Sussex Drip Pudding or Plum Heavies, for instance. (Plum Heavy is perhaps

More than one Sussex village has a reputation for not shutting doors, but Yapton is probably the best known. One reason for Yapton's pre-eminence was said to be that leaving their doors open made it easier for smugglers to pass through the village; another involves the Yapton farmer whose cow caught her head between the bars of a gate. The farmer had to saw her head off and ever after kept all his gates permanently open.

The Horsham town stocks, photographed in 1859. Contrary to the fears expressed in the caption, they were not destroyed, but reappeared close to their original site, on the Carfax, in the 1930s, before finally coming to rest in the local museum. Charles Price's incarceration took place around 1830.

THE HORSHAM STOCKS.

These stocks stood on the Carfax, near the site of the present Bandstand, and were used for minor offences, chiefly drunkenness, &c., the helpless offender being taunted and jeered by the onlookers, and no doubt in many cases was made a target for those of a sporting turn. The stocks were discovered in 1859 in the Fire Engine-house, then situated near Manor-place, and were taken out and photographed, the old Horshamites sitting in them to illustrate their use. What ultimately became of them is not clear, but possibly they were burnt on a 5th of November.

Last man actually in the stocks, Charles Price, a local bun man.

the most famous of all Sussex recipes: the name has even been used for the title of a Sussex magazine.) Others have place-names in their titles. So here is a selection of traditional Sussex recipes:

SUSSEX PLUM HEAVIES or PLUM DUFFS

2 oz lard	*2 oz currants or sultanas*
2 cups flour	*1 cup of milk, soured by adding juice of*
1 oz castor sugar	*half a lemon*

Rub the lard into the flour. Add sugar and fruit, then the soured milk, to make the mixture into pastry. Roll out and cut into small rounds. Brush over with the rest of the milk, then bake for 15 minutes in a moderate oven.

SUSSEX POND PUDDING or BLACKEYED SUSAN or WELL PUDDING

This was traditionally eaten on Palm Sunday and was sometimes called Palm Pudding.

Suet dough	*Brown sugar*
4 oz butter	*Spice*
Handful currants	

Roll out a large piece of suet dough into a thick, round shape about the size of a dinner plate. In the centre, place a large ball of butter, the currants and sugar and a pinch of spice. Pull the suet crust up round the butter ball until the pudding looks like a large apple dumpling. Seal the top with a piece of suet crust. Tie in a floured cloth and boil for $2-2\frac{1}{2}$ hours.

In some recipes, the currants are put into the dough. When serving, cut a slice off the top. Some cooks suggest that, before serving, you should cut a round hole in the middle and stir in some home-made wine or sherry with brown sugar. Another variation is to put a lemon, pricked all over, into the centre of the ball of butter.

SUSSEX DRIPPED (or DRIP or DROP) PUDDING

This is a pudding to eat with your Sunday roast. Just as Yorkshire has its pudding, so does Sussex, but in our case it is a suet pudding rather than a batter. You can always tell a true Sussex man by asking him if he was brought up to eat Dripped Pudding with the Sunday joint.

6 oz suet	*Teaspoon baking powder*
1 lb plain flour	*Pinch of salt*

Shred the suet and mix with the flour, baking powder and salt, adding about $\frac{1}{2}$ pint of cold water to form a suet roly-poly. Tie into floured cloth and boil for 1 hour. Remove from the cloth and cut into slices. Lay these in the dripping pan beneath the roasting meat, so that they become saturated with the dripping

The contrast between town and country was marked even in the comparatively peaceful Sussex of seventy years ago, as these two photographs, taken within a few miles of each other, show. *Above:* Falmer village. *Below:* the London Road, Brighton. The tramlines caused the downfall (or embarrassing rerouting) of many a cyclist and, later, motorcyclist and in 1926 motorcycle tyres were made wider specifically to overcome the problem. Brighton Corporation trams ran from 1901 until 1939, when they were replaced for a time by the less noisy but more mundane trolley bus.

and brown on top. Alternatively, the meat may be removed from the pan a few minutes before serving and the slices of pudding thoroughly coated or 'dropped' in the hot dripping. If desired, continue cooking for a short while so that the slices become brown and crunchy.

Sometimes, this pudding was served as a separate course just before the meat and vegetables. Sultanas may be added to the pudding, if you wish. This recipe reached my wife via my mother and grandmother. They both favoured the method of putting the pudding slices in the dripping after the meat had been removed.

HARD DUMPLINGS

Flour   *Water*
Salt

Make a paste or light dough from the flour, salt and water. Shape into balls or large sausages and dust with flour. Boil for nearly 1 hour. When cooked, they can be cut into slices about 1 inch thick and placed in the dripping pan under your roasting meat for 20–30 minutes before it is dished up. It is said that only a Sussex woman can make these hard dumplings successfully.

(From Worthing, 1822. Originally printed in *Good Things in England*, ed. Florence White, Jonathan Cape, 1933: now available in paperback, published by Futura Books. Reprinted by permission.)

SUSSEX MEAT PUDDING

Suet dough   *Bay leaf*
Steak and kidney   *Mushrooms*

Make a meat pudding as usual, but place a bay leaf and one or two mushrooms on top of the meat before the lid of suet crust is put on. Another version has the meat pudding flavoured with truffles, giving the gravy a rich and almost black appearance. (Truffles, sometimes called ground mushrooms, were once very popular in Sussex. My father remembers digging for them as a boy. Now they seem to have disappeared.)

SUSSEX SAVOURY DUMPLINGS

$\frac{1}{2}$ *lb flour*   *1 teaspoon mixed herbs*
$\frac{1}{4}$ *lb suet*   *Pepper and salt*
$\frac{1}{4}$ *lb any cold meat, diced*   *1 egg*

Mix ingredients together, then add a well-beaten egg and a little water. Roll into dumplings and boil for 15 minutes. Serve with gravy.

SUSSEX BACON PUDDING, NO. 1

Suet dough   *Sage and seasoning*

| Chopped bacon | Swede |
| Onion | Turnips |

Roll out firm dough thinly and spread with chopped bacon, onion, sage and seasoning. Roll it over and over, as for jam roly-poly. Tie in a cloth. Boil surrounded by swedes and turnips. (Sausage meat may be substituted for bacon, if desired.)

SUSSEX BACON PUDDING, NO. 2

Suet dough	Pepper and salt
3 or 4 rashers of bacon	Mixed herbs
1 onion	1 egg
Parsley	Milk

Line a greased basin with the suet dough. Beat the egg well. Chop the bacon, onion and parsley and mix in well, with a little salt and pepper, a teaspoon of mixed herbs, the egg and a little milk. Place in the basin and cover with a lid of dough. Boil for 2 hours. Serve with a thick gravy. (Sausage meat may be substituted for the bacon.)

CHIDDINGLY HOT POT

1 lb beef	1 lb onions or shallots
8 oz celery	1 lb potatoes
8 oz olives	Cloves
Tarragon vinegar	Black peppercorns
Mixed spices	

Chop onions, celery and olives. Place a layer of onions on the bottom of a large casserole dish, with some of the olives and celery. Put thin slices of beef on top of them and sprinkle with a little spice and vinegar. Cut potatoes into thin slices and place over the meat, with some more olives and celery. Repeat until all the ingredients are used up. Pour enough water into the casserole to nearly cover. Cook in a low oven for 3–4 hours, according to quantities used. The vinegar renders salt unnecessary.

(From E. Manvel, of Broadbridge Heath.)

WINDMILL HILL THIN BISCUITS

| 2 handfuls flour | Butter, walnut-sized lump |
| Pinch of salt | ½ small teaspoon baking powder |

Rub ingredients together well and add milk to make a stiff paste. Roll out very thin and bake.

(Published in *Sussex County Magazine*, vol. 10.)

SUSSEX CAKES (or LARDY JOHNS)

$\frac{1}{4}$ *lb lard*
$\frac{1}{2}$ *lb flour*
1 oz sugar

2 level teaspoons baking powder
1 oz currants

Rub the lard into the flour. Add sugar and baking powder. Stir in the currants with 1 gill of water. Mix all to a stiff dough. Roll out and cut into squares. Bake in a quick oven for about 20 minutes.

(From Miss K. Effinger, of East Worthing. She was given this recipe many years ago by a lady of ninety-seven.)

COAGER (pronounced *cojer*) CAKES

The name is possibly a corruption of 'cold cheer'. It once meant a cold meal eaten by farm workers at eleven or twelve o'clock.

Pastry
Butter

Sugar
Sultanas

To use up left-over pastry from pie-making, roll out pastry into thin rounds about $2\frac{1}{2}$ inches across. In the middle, put a knob of butter, a half teaspoon of sugar and a few sultanas. Catch it all up round to the middle, press top and add a little bit of pastry. Bake in the normal way. My mother always made these, but without giving them a name. Another recipe suggests adding pieces of fat salt pork.

SUSSEX CURRANT AND APPLE DUMPLINGS

$\frac{1}{2}$ *lb flour*
$\frac{1}{2}$ *lb suet*
2 oz sugar
2 oz currants

1 ripe apple, peeled, cored and diced
Pinch of salt
Sour milk

Mix ingredients together with a little water. Roll into dumplings. Boil for 15 minutes. Dust with moist sugar and serve with treacle.

SUSSEX TRUG.

5

Guy Fawkes, Old Clem and Sussex Witches

5 NOVEMBER, Bonfire or Guy Fawkes Night, has always been very important in Sussex. Of course, bonfires were popular long before the Gunpowder Plot, but the custom, with its anti-Popery overtones, became focused on this day.

Lewes is the most famous place in Sussex for Bonfire Night celebrations and has several rival Bonfire Societies. Nowadays, there are processions, with gaudy costumes and flamboyant banners, but the celebrations were once even more abandoned and over the years several strong measures had to be taken by the authorities to curb them. George Townsend, of Lewes, remembered when soldiers were brought into the town to stop the Bonfire Boys from throwing blazing tar barrels down the High Street. He also remembered, although not present himself, that the Riot Act was read by the Lord Lieutenant of the county.

In Horsham, even as late as 1922, someone could write: 'From the window of 48 West Street I have many times watched the procession of grotesque figures, the whole scene lighted with red, blue and green Roman candles. Afterwards, stood in the Carfax and watched the big fire and the burning of the guys.'

Horsham Carfax was *the* place for public events, such as fairs and bonfires, and nearby houses and shops often had their paint scorched by particularly big fires. Like wassailing and similar customs, bonfires were yet another excuse for knocking on doors and soliciting pennies. Before 1900, it was the accepted thing for boys to dress up in paper hats, blacken their faces and call on residents, singing their bonfire song and blowing cow horns.

23 November, the feast of St Clement, who was martyred by being thrown into the sea tied to an anchor, is known in Sussex as Old Clem Night. St Clement is the patron saint of blacksmiths (although some people might feel it should be St Dunstan, who was well known in Sussex folklore as a blacksmith).

Mr Laker, of Brighton, told me when he was seventy-nine: 'In Storrington (when I was at school), the village blacksmith used to fire his anvil and then have supper in the evening at the Anchor. They used to call it 'Old Clem Night'. My father and uncle used to go each year. After the corn-sowing season

87

was over, they also had bread and cheese given them (the carters) by the village blacksmith.'

'Firing the anvil' meant filling and plugging the hole beneath the blacksmith's anvil, where it was fixed to the block, with gunpowder. A trail of powder was then laid and lighted with a heated rod. The firing of the anvil was used to celebrate not only Old Clem Night but many other events. It was fired at Storrington on Mafeking Night, for instance, and at Billingshurst for the Relief of Ladysmith. Other Boer War victories were similarly marked, as was the end of the 1914–18 war. In 1912, the vicar of Kirdford had the anvil fired on the occasion of his daughter's marriage, and it was also fired to celebrate such events as the twenty-first birthday of the local squire's son.

It sounds rather a dangerous operation, and such it sometimes proved. On one occasion, when a blacksmith was giving the plug a final blow, it went off prematurely, blew the axe out of his hand, stripped him of his shirt and blew gunpowder into his arms and hair.

A Worthing man in his eighties told me of the last time the anvil was fired there, for the coronation of Edward VII. He also remembered it being fired on Mafeking Night – and hiding because the explosion frightened him so!

In some places, an effigy of Old Clem was made, a figure with a wig, beard and pipe. This was then set up over the door of the inn where the blacksmith's feast was to be held. Sometimes, after the boys had made their effigy, they would put him in a chair and carry him round the houses, begging apples and

This Bonfire Society at Brighton was one of many which flourished years ago. Sussex has always been noted for keeping up the traditions of 5 November and Lewes still transforms itself from a sedate, old-fashioned town into a scene of almost pagan abandon.

Not all effigies on Bonfire Night were of Guy Fawkes. Here, an unpopular Chancellor gets the treatment at Bucks Green in 1909. Perhaps this is a tradition which should not have been allowed to die out!

beer. At Brighton, the blacksmith's feast consisted of a 'Way Goose', which was not a goose at all, but a leg of pork, boned and stuffed with sage and onions. The song the smiths sang at their feast was traditionally *Twankydillo*.

Firing the anvil was revived at Pyecombe in 1962.

25 November, St Catherine's Day, was often linked with St Clement's Day. Children went round asking for food and singing:

> *Catternen' and Clemen' be here, here, here.*
> *Give us your apples and give us your pears,*
> *One for Peter, two for Paul,*
> *Three for Him who made us all.*
> *Clemen' was a good man,*
> *Cattern' was his mother,*
> *And may God give your soul good rest.*

This was particularly a children's custom and was known as 'Catterning and Clemening'.

◇ ◇ ◇

Winter evenings are the times to think and talk about supernatural beings – ghosts, fairies and witches. Ghost stories we will leave until Christmas, and the fairies we have already talked about. That leaves witches, and there were quite a number in Sussex at one time. Yet we seem to have behaved fairly tolerantly towards them. Of eighteen alleged witches brought to trial in Sussex between 1559 and 1701, only four were actually found guilty and only one hanged. That unfortunate was Margaret Cooper, of Kirdford, who was accused of bewitching three people, causing them to die. She was hanged at Horsham. The last trial for witchcraft in Sussex took place at Horsham, too, in 1680.

Old women believed to be witches probably fell into two categories: those who were old, ugly, deformed or half-witted – or perhaps all four – who because of their oddities were feared by their neighbours; and genuinely evil women who enjoyed the sense of power which the reputation of being a witch gave them. Some probably believed in their own supernatural powers.

Witches were popularly supposed to have the power of turning themselves into animals. A witch named Dame Garson, when chased by the hounds while in the form of a hare, jumped safely through the window of her cottage, crying, 'Ah, my boys, you ain't got me yet!' A hare was a popular disguise. Sometimes, the story goes, the hounds almost caught the hare, but lost it again after it had been injured; later, the witch would be seen limping . . .

Some witches were supposed to have power over horses and to be able to hold them up or stop them working. As abnormal power over horses is not unknown even today, perhaps such claims were not so far-fetched.

Charms were often employed against witches, and old kitchen vessels are

PRICE SIXPENCE   1606—1958

CLIFFE BONFIRE SOCIETY

"Nulli Secundus"

SOUVENIR and PROGRAMME

Photograph by courtesy of Reeves Studios, 150 High Street, Lewes

353rd ANNIVERSARY

of the discovery of the Gunpowder Plot, and the

270th ANNIVERSARY

of the landing of William, Prince of Orange

WEDNESDAY, NOVEMBER 5th, 1958

Headquarters : "DORSET ARMS."

OUR CAUSE IS JUST — AND MUST PREVAIL

Compare this 1958 programme of the Cliffe Bonfire Society, of Lewes, with the 1873 programme following.

sometimes found bearing 'witches' marks', thought to be charms to keep witches at bay. A certain way to detect a witch was to snip off a piece of her hair so that it fell into a pot of boiling water. As the hair entered the water, the witch would scream.

Witches in Sussex were male or female, the term wizard being almost unknown. The males tended to be more often of the White variety, as indeed some of the females undoubtedly were. They were wise men, or women, who made themselves useful to the community with their knowledge of simple medicine, veterinary skills or the ability, for instance, to divine water or metal. Witches were supposed always to hand their knowledge on to someone before they died, and probably much of the useful knowledge of the wise woman had been passed on to her by her mother. The saying was, 'You should not eat or drink with a witch, or it will give her power over you.' Someone once told me that his mother annoyed the other women of the village by remaining on friendly terms with a wizened old lady who was thought to be one of the several witches in the district.

◇ ◇ ◇

But dark winter evenings were also the time for other stories. We have a tremendous sense of humour in Sussex, although strangers may not always be aware of it. Our humour is of the quiet, sly kind that sneaks up on you when you are least expecting it, often by a neat sting in the end of a story. Our humorists usually operate with a perfectly serious expression and this makes the shock of being 'kidded' even greater. We don't go in for huge belly laughs; a grin or a chuckle is the most you will normally get out of a true Sussex countryman. But please don't assume that the humour is under-developed or lacking in any way. Some of our humour is extremely deep and thought-provoking.

The Sussex man does not like to be laughed at; it offends his natural dignity. However, he will often poke fun at other people, particularly if they come from another county. But usually the fun is of a gentle kind and the sting, if sting there be, is only apparent after some consideration of what has been said.

Even today, we have our country comedians. I recall coming home late one night on top of a Southdown bus from Brighton. Two Sussex men kept the whole deck delighted by their continuous repartee, delivered in soft country accents. Most of the jokes had seen many years' service and were obviously old friends, but nobody minded. 'What did you give your cow when it was sick?' 'Turpentine.' A week later: 'I did like you said and gave my cow turpentine, but it died.' 'That's funny, so did mine.' They must have done it many times

Commercial Square Bonfire Society's Bonfire Night programme for 1873. A 'new banneret' proclaimed, 'Girls, be true to your Bonfire Boys'. (*Reproduced by permission of East Sussex County Library.*)

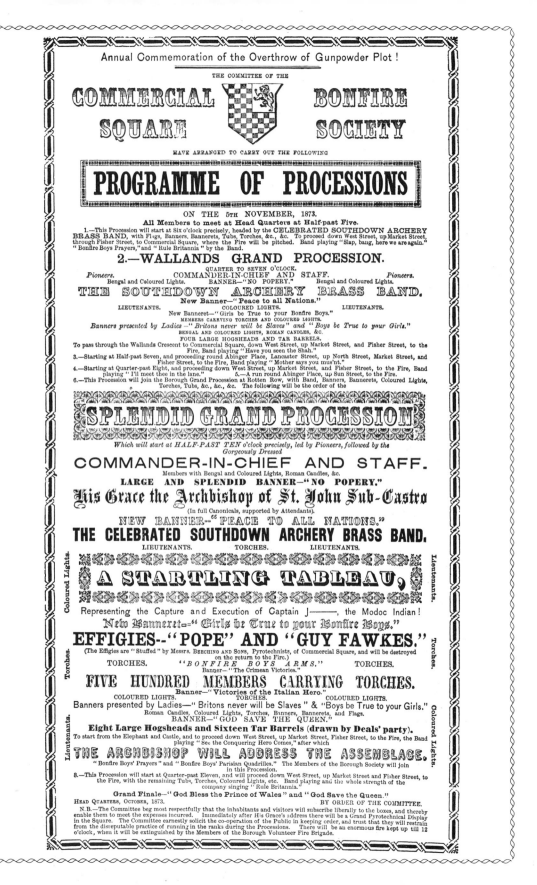

Annual Commemoration of the Overthrow of Gunpowder Plot!

THE COMMITTEE OF THE

COMMERCIAL SQUARE BONFIRE SOCIETY

HAVE ARRANGED TO CARRY OUT THE FOLLOWING

PROGRAMME OF PROCESSIONS

ON THE 5TH NOVEMBER, 1873.

All Members to meet at Head Quarters at Half-past Five.

1.—This Procession will start at Six o'clock precisely, headed by the CELEBRATED SOUTHDOWN ARCHERY BRASS BAND, with Flags, Banners, Bannerets, Tubs, Torches, &c., &c. To proceed down West Street, up Market Street, through Fisher Street, to Commercial Square, where the Fire will be pitched. Band playing "Slap, bang, here we are again." "Bonfire Boys Prayers," and "Rule Britannia" by the Band.

2.—WALLANDS GRAND PROCESSION.

QUARTER TO SEVEN O'CLOCK.

Pioneers. COMMANDER-IN-CHIEF AND STAFF. *Pioneers.*

Bengal and Coloured Lights. BANNER—"NO POPERY." Bengal and Coloured Lights.

THE SOUTHDOWN ARCHERY BRASS BAND.

New Banner—"Peace to all Nations."

LIEUTENANTS. COLOURED LIGHTS. LIEUTENANTS.

New Banneret—"Girls be True to your Bonfire Boys."

MEMBERS CARRYING TORCHES AND COLOURED LIGHTS.

Banners presented by Ladies—"Britons never will be Slaves" and "Boys be True to your Girls."

BENGAL AND COLOURED LIGHTS, ROMAN CANDLES, &C.

FOUR LARGE HOGSHEADS AND TAR BARRELS.

To pass through the Wallands Crescent to Commercial Square, down West Street, up Market Street, and Fisher Street, to the Fire, Band playing "Have you seen the Shah."

3.—Starting at Half-past Seven, and proceeding round Abinger Place, Lancaster Street, up North Street, Market Street, and Fisher Street, to the Fire, Band playing "Mother says you mus'nt."

4.—Starting at Quarter-past Eight, and proceeding down West Street, up Market Street, and Fisher Street, to the Fire, Band playing "I'll meet thee in the lane."

5.—A run round Abinger Place, up Sun Street, to the Fire.

6.—This Procession will join the Borough Grand Procession at Rotten Row, with Band, Banners, Bannerets, Coloured Lights, Torches, Tubs, &c., &c., &c. The following will be the order of the

SPLENDID GRAND PROCESSION

Which will start at HALF-PAST TEN o'clock precisely, led by Pioneers, followed by the Gorgeously Dressed

COMMANDER-IN-CHIEF AND STAFF.

Members with Bengal and Coloured Lights, Roman Candles, &c.

LARGE AND SPLENDID BANNER—"NO POPERY."

His Grace the Archbishop of St. John Sub-Castro

(In full Canonicals, supported by Attendants).

NEW BANNER—"PEACE TO ALL NATIONS."

THE CELEBRATED SOUTHDOWN ARCHERY BRASS BAND.

LIEUTENANTS. TORCHES. LIEUTENANTS.

Coloured Lights. Lieutenants.

A STARTLING TABLEAU,

Representing the Capture and Execution of Captain J——, the Modoc Indian!

New Banneret—"Girls be True to your Bonfire Boys."

EFFIGIES—"POPE" AND "GUY FAWKES."

(The Effigies are "Stuffed" by Messrs. BEECHING AND SONS, Pyrotechnists, of Commercial Square, and will be destroyed on the return to the Fire.)

Torches. Torches.

TORCHES. *"BONFIRE BOYS ARMS."* TORCHES.

Banner—"The Crimean Victories."

FIVE HUNDRED MEMBERS CARRYING TORCHES.

Banner—"Victories of the Italian Hero."

COLOURED LIGHTS. TORCHES. COLOURED LIGHTS.

Banners presented by Ladies—"Britons never will be Slaves" & "Boys be True to your Girls."

Roman Candles, Coloured Lights, Torches, Banners, Bannerets, and Flags.

BANNER—"GOD SAVE THE QUEEN."

Eight Large Hogsheads and Sixteen Tar Barrels (drawn by Deals' party).

To start from the Elephant and Castle, and to proceed down West Street, up Market Street, Fisher Street, to the Fire, the Band playing "See the Conquering Hero Comes," after which

Lieutenants. Coloured Lights.

THE ARCHBISHOP WILL ADDRESS THE ASSEMBLAGE.

"Bonfire Boys' Prayers" and "Bonfire Boys' Parisian Quadrilles." The Members of the Borough Society will join in this Procession.

8.—This Procession will start at Quarter-past Eleven, and will proceed down West Street, up Market Street and Fisher Street, to the Fire, with the remaining Tubs, Torches, Coloured Lights, etc. Band playing and the whole strength of the company singing "Rule Britannia."

Grand Finale—"God Bless the Prince of Wales" and "God Save the Queen."

HEAD QUARTERS, OCTOBER, 1873. BY ORDER OF THE COMMITTEE.

N.B.—The Committee beg most respectfully that the inhabitants and visitors will subscribe liberally to the boxes, and thereby enable them to meet the expenses incurred. Immediately after His Grace's address there will be a Grand Pyrotechnical Display in the Square. The Committee earnestly solicit the co-operation of the Public in keeping order, and trust that they will restrain from the disreputable practice of running in the ranks during the Processions. There will be an enormous fire kept up till 12 o'clock, when it will be extinguished by the Members of the Borough Volunteer Fire Brigade.

before – it was just too good to be completely impromptu – but it didn't sound at all rehearsed or prearranged.

Tall tales take their place in the repertoire of Sussex humour, as in all country communities. They are particularly popular if they are aimed at townsmen. Here is a typical example: a poacher went out with a catapult and when he saw a hare he looked round for a suitable stone. Failing to find one, he took a piece of cobbler's wax from his pocket, softened it in his mouth and shot with it, hitting the hare neatly between the eyes. The hare ran across the field and met another head-on. The two stuck fast together, thus enabling the poacher to bag two hares instead of one.

Here is another: a farmer was out with his scythe one day. Unfortunately, he misjudged his stroke and cut his little dog neatly down the middle. With great presence of mind, he clapped the two halves together. But in his haste he stuck one side on the wrong way up. Forever afterwards, the poor dog had to run somersault fashion, first with his two right legs and then with his two left legs.

Here is one of those stories in which the simple Sussex countryman outwits authority: a drover was caught by a policeman sleeping in a haystack. He descended by means of a ladder and said to the constable, 'What about my wife and children up there?' The constable went up the ladder to look, whereupon the drover took the ladder away and made his escape.

Here is one from Henry Burstow, of Horsham: there was an old man and an old woman. They had a son and his name was Jack. The old man died and the old woman married again. Jack didn't like his new 'father', so he ran away. When he found he couldn't better himself, he came home again and knocked at his mother's door. 'Who's there?' asked the old woman. 'It's me, Jack.' 'And where have you been to?' 'I've been to heaven to see your old husband.' 'Oh lor, and how is he?' 'He's very well and only wants two things to make him completely happy. That's five pounds and the old grey mare.' 'You go and get the mare, Jack, and I'll give you the money.' So Jack gets the mare and the money and off he goes. Along the road, he meets a shepherd. He says, 'You mind, Master, telling a lie for once?' 'No, not if I'm well paid for it.' 'If anyone asks you if you've seen me, you tell them you see me fly right up into the sky.' And Jack gave the shepherd a shilling for his trouble. (The story continues in song, with the shepherd effectively pulling the wool over the stepfather's eyes.)

Monologues were once very popular as country entertainment. Richard Lower, of Chiddingly, who was noted for his Sussex dialect writings, was the author of two long monologues written in 'pure Sussex doggerel'. The best known is *Tom Cladpole's Jurney to Lunnon, told by myself*. The other is *Jan Cladpole's trip to 'Merricur in search of Dollar Trees*. They were both published in Lewes and my copy of the second bears the printed price, 6d. Both the wanderers returned gladly home, incidentally. The 'trip to Lunnon' ends with Tom declaring:

The Motor·Car·Accident -at·the·Bottom·of·Rowhook·Hill·on·July·25·1908

Early road accidents in Sussex involving mechanised vehicles. Road accidents were sufficiently rare to inspire picture postcards of them (*above*, 'The Motor Car Accident' at Rowhook Hill, carefully dated).

This steamroller in the ditch at Slinfold must have posed a problem. Did they bring another steam engine along to haul it out – or were the steamer's old rivals, the horses, persuaded to rescue it?

Fer I have larn't a thing or two,
From what I now have sin:
An wise anuf I'm sartin sure,
Never to goo agin!

My friend Cyril Phillips, who once farmed at Firle, has written a monologue based on the legend of the Wilmington Giant, as told by a one-armed shepherd who tended his flock on the Downs near Alfriston in the 1920s. The story was that there were originally two giants: one lived on the Caburn and the other on Windover. Their work was flint-cracking, and while they worked with their hammers they shouted to each other across the four miles separating them. One day, they had an argument and the Mount Caburn Hill giant threw his hammer at his friend, meaning merely to hurt him. He scored a direct hit, however, and they buried the dead giant just where he lay: and that's his outline you can see there today.

———

Sussex wines and other drinks

To add to our enjoyment of long winter evenings, we must have something to drink. Sussex people make hundreds of different kinds of drink. Indeed, it is said we will make wine out of almost anything. Here are just a few recipes:

POTATO WINE

½ *gal small potatoes*	*3 lb granulated sugar*
1 gal cold water	*2 oranges*
3 pieces root ginger	*2 lemons*

Wash the potatoes and cut them in half. Put into a pan with the water and root ginger. Bring to the boil, then boil for 10 minutes. Slice the oranges and lemons and place with the sugar into another pan. Strain the potato water on to the fruit mixture and boil again for 30 minutes. Bottle when cold and cork tightly once the wine has finished working. (No yeast needed.)

Warn anyone to whom you give this wine (as my mother always did) that it is very potent and should be treated with great respect.

ELDERBERRY WINE

1 gal elderberries	*3 lb sugar*
1 gal water	

Strip the elderberries from their stems, add water and boil for 15 minutes. Strain and throw pulp away. Add sugar and leave to ferment for 14 days, then skim and bottle. Keep 1 year.

The village blacksmith at Chailey Green early this century. In the years that followed, the mechanisation of the farm brought a sharp decline in the number of working smiths. But now that riding schools and leisure riding are both so popular, new men are taking up this ancient trade.

Because of the fire, the village smithy (this one was at Poynings) was the meeting-place of the old or the unemployed – and the smith was sometimes glad of an extra pair of hands.

TREACLE BEER

1 lb treacle   *Teacup of yeast*

Put the treacle into 2 quarts of boiling water. Mix and add 8 quarts of cold water and the yeast. Put into a cask for 2 or 3 days. Then bottle.
(Published in *The Mistress of Stanton's Farm*, Marcus Woodward, 1938.)

CIDER WINE

7 lb small apples   *1 gal water*
3½ lb sugar

Leave the skin on and cut up the apples. Cover with water and leave to stand for 21 days, squeezing and stirring every day. Then strain. Add sugar to the liquid and stir till dissolved. Put in a warm place and leave to ferment for 3 weeks, then skim and bottle, but do not cork too tightly for a time.

BEETROOT WINE

1 gal water   *Juice of 3 lemons*
4 lb beetroot   *8 cloves*
4 lb sugar

Wash the beetroot and cut up quickly into the water. Boil for 20 minutes, then strain. Add sugar and lemon juice while hot. Stir until sugar dissolves. Add cloves. Leave to ferment for 3 weeks, then skim, strain and bottle.

HUCKLE–MY–BLUFF

This is the Sussex name for egg-flip, with the addition of beer to the brandy and eggs.
(From E. Manvel, of Broadbridge Heath.)

DONKEY TEA

Toast slices of bread until well burnt. Break into pieces and put into teapot. Pour boiling water over the pieces. Drink when cold. (A really 'hard times' drink. I haven't had the courage to try it!)

NETTLE BEER

2 gal nettle leaves   *1 lb lump sugar for each gallon*
Juice of 1 lemon   *Yeast*

Pick the nettle leaves in the spring. Add the rind of a lemon and enough water to cover them. Boil for 5 minutes, then strain. Add the 1 lb of sugar to each gallon of liquor, plus the lemon juice. Spread yeast on a piece of toast, place it on top of the liquid when cool and leave for 24 hours. Lift off the toast. Bottle, but do not cork too tightly until working has finished.

BALM WINE

5 lb sugar
½ lb balm leaves

Yeast
Sugar lumps

Boil the sugar in 9 pints of water for 1 hour. Then put into crock to cool. Squeeze balm leaves together to bruise them, then place them into the crock, stirring them round with a small quantity of yeast. Cover the crock. Stir each day, keeping the crock uncovered after the first day. When the wine has stopped working, cover and, after six weeks, bottle. Put a lump of sugar into each bottle.

SYLLABUB

1 pint of port
1 pint sherry or other white wine
Sugar
Milk

Clotted cream
Nutmeg
Cinnamon

Put the port and sherry into a china bowl and add sugar to taste. Fill up the bowl with milk. After 20 minutes, cover with the clotted cream and grate the nutmeg and cinnamon over it.

(Published in *The Mistress of Stanton's Farm*, Marcus Woodward, 1938.)

Mince Pies, Mummers and Mistletoe

21 DECEMBER is the shortest day of the year and St Thomas's Day. The Yule Log was brought indoors on this day in readiness for burning during the twelve days of Christmas. After Twelfth Night, the last piece of the log was carefully preserved until the following year, to act as kindling for a new log. This meant good luck within the house for the whole year – and ensured the continuity of one more traditional custom.

There were several superstitions connected with the burning of the Yule Log. For instance, if a person with a squint, or someone barefooted, came to the house while the log was burning, this was considered unlucky.

The feast of St Thomas was also the day when poorer folk went 'a-goodening'. It was a day when, traditionally, no one refused a caller who asked for a gift. It was the women who usually visited the big houses, many of which gave generously. One man always gave a halfpenny candle, another a reel of cotton. Widows received double. Originally, the monks and churches were the main benefactors, but by the nineteenth century it was the big houses of the area who assumed this charitable duty. Many poor people would have had a meagre Christmas dinner without this custom, which included the giving of joints of meat, plum puddings and tea. Even local shops joined in, sometimes putting boxes of goods outside for those who came 'a-goodening'.

Henry Burstow, in his *Reminiscences of Horsham*, speaks of 26 December as 'Gooding Day', possibly a confusion with Boxing Day. He well recalled the customs associated with it. He remembered that Sir Timothy Shelley, of Field Place, used to give away beef in large quantities. Mr R. Aldridge, of St Leonards, gave about 6 lb of beef and a Christmas pudding each to about sixty families and Mrs Fox, of Chestnut Lodge, gave $\frac{1}{4}$ lb of tea and 2s. 6d. in cash to about eighty old women and one shilling in cash to two hundred more.

Earlier in the nineteenth century, Phoebe Hessel, the famous Brighton character who went to the wars disguised as a man, regularly kept up the custom of 'goodening' on St Thomas's Day. Each year, she made a point of visiting her well-to-do friends, regaling them with her memories in return for fruit cake and wine.

Chart's Corn Stores, in North Street, Horsham, around 1910. 'Father Chart' is standing in the doorway. As well as using his cart to deliver coal, he gave rides to local children. When he died, they gladly offered a prayer for him each day in school: 'Our Father Chart in heaven . . .' The shop survives, though it is no longer a corn store. The name lives on, too, in a new road behind the shop, Chart Way.

The sweet shop which stood opposite Mr Chart's stores. Sweets were sold loose, in paper cones deftly fashioned by the shopkeeper. Note the advertisement for R. White's Ginger Beer at one penny a bottle, and the confidently permanent-looking signs, all hand-painted.

Phoebe Hessel

Like so many others which had not lapsed before, the custom disappeared around the time of the First World War, 1922 being the last year in which I can find any record of it. Nowadays, the Christmas cheer dispensed to the poor and elderly by such organisations as Rotary takes the place of the old personal giving.

One further custom associated with 21 December: if a girl wished to dream of her future lover, she had to peel an onion and place it on a handkerchief under her pillow when she went to bed, reciting these words:

> *Good St Thomas, do me right,*
> *And see my true love comes tonight,*
> *In the clothes and in the array*
> *That he weareth every day.*

◇ ◇ ◇

We are fortunate in Sussex in having two of our own Christmas carols. One is the well known 'Sussex Carol', which begins, *On Christmas night all Christians sing.* This was collected by Ralph Vaughan Williams (who did a lot of his song-collecting in Sussex) from Mr and Mrs Verrall, in Horsham, on 24 May 1904. The Verralls lived in North Street, Horsham, but had previously lived at Monks Gate. It was there that Vaughan Williams collected the folk song, *Our Captain Calls All Hands*, the tune of which he called 'Monks Gate' and which he used for the Pilgrims' Hymn, *He Who Would Valiant Be.*

Our other Sussex carol is the 'Sussex Mummers' Carol', included in a collection by another well known folk song collector, Lucy Broadwood, who lived near Rusper. The carol as it was remembered was actually the result of a folk song competition run by the *West Sussex Gazette* in 1905. It had been last sung in 1881, when the mummers – or tipteers, as they were known in Sussex – gave the last performance of their traditional play in the vicinity of Horsham.

The script of this particular play, *St George and the Turk*, eventually found

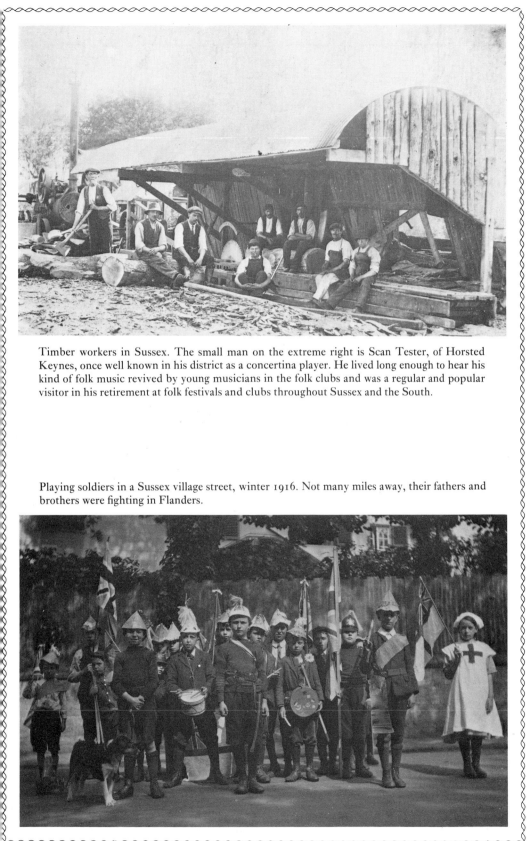

Timber workers in Sussex. The small man on the extreme right is Scan Tester, of Horsted Keynes, once well known in his district as a concertina player. He lived long enough to hear his kind of folk music revived by young musicians in the folk clubs and was a regular and popular visitor in his retirement at folk festivals and clubs throughout Sussex and the South.

Playing soldiers in a Sussex village street, winter 1916. Not many miles away, their fathers and brothers were fighting in Flanders.

its way into the Vaughan Williams Memorial Library at Cecil Sharp House, London, along with other manuscripts from Lucy Broadwood's collection. When the Horsham Morris dancers, the Broadwood Men (named in honour of Lucy Broadwood), wanted to revive the play, they were able to obtain the words from the Cecil Sharp library and thus resuscitate a tradition which had been interrupted towards the end of the last century.

The 1880 mummers wore dresses of coloured calico and old 'chimney-pot' hats, heavily trimmed with shreds of ribbon, gaudy paper fringes and ornaments. The present-day mummers do their best to live up to the standards set by their grandfathers, and each Christmas their play is performed on Boxing Day around Horsham and Rusper, including the Carfax, the centre of Horsham. Of course, they conclude in the correct manner with the singing of the 'Sussex Mummers' Carol'.

Once, almost every country village had its own mumming play. In Sussex, about forty have been noted and more must have been lost without trace. The most usual characters in these plays, which were normally performed in the South of England around Christmas and the New Year, were St George (or King George), the Turkish Knight, the Doctor, Father Christmas and Beelzebub. Subsidiary characters were introduced from time to time and for a period a topical hero might be substituted for a traditional one: Nelson or Napoleon, for example.

None of these plays has survived in an unbroken tradition in Sussex, although there have been several revivals, many of them in recent years. (We shouldn't forget the Boxgrove Tipteers, a revival team of the 1920s, who also sang carols and folk songs, including *The Moon Shone Bright* and *Sweet Rosy Morn*, and performed the dance, 'Over the Sticks'.)

One of the first of the modern revivals was the Steyning Play, which has now been performed for several years by the Chanctonbury Ring Morris Men. Originally, they performed it every Boxing Day outside the White Horse at Steyning, but now they do it elsewhere in the district. They also take the play out on New Year's Day, now that this is a public holiday.

The name 'tipteers' (or 'tipteerers', as it is sometimes used) has so far defied folklorists to discover a satisfactory origin.

George Attrill, the Fittleworth folk singer and character, gave me the script of the Fittleworth Play, which was known as *King George and the Dragon*. The Fittleworth cast consisted of Father Christmas, Billy Twing Twang, King George, the Turkish Knight, the Valiant Soldier, the Doctor and the Prince of Peace. The Prince of Peace was actually a second appearance of Father Christmas. In spite of the title, there was no dragon.

George said that the players always used to be known as tipteers and that 'mummers' was a more modern name. At Christmas, they used to go round the houses and ask if they might come in and perform their play. When it was over,

'Tipteerers' play at Chithurst. The photograph is undated, but the play probably died out soon after 1912. The characters are Father Christmas (centre), Jolly John, Gallant Soldier, King George IV, Turkish Knight, Noble Captain and Doctor Good. *(Photograph: University of Reading Museum of English Rural Life.)*

A quoits team from the Barley Mow pub at Selmeston. Quoits, once a popular game in Sussex, virtually died out between the wars. As far as I know, it is now played at only one place in the county – the Victory pub at Staplefield, where a game takes place each Boxing Day.

they would be given a few pence and a drink. By the end of the day, they would be 'somewhat under the weather'.

The 1914 war killed the Fittleworth Play, but it was revived for the jubilee of King George V and again later for special occasions. In the revival, George played Father Christmas.

This is the script he showed me:

King George and the Dragon

Mummers' play as performed in the Fittleworth area

FATHER CHRISTMAS: In comes I, old Father Christmas, am I welcome or am I not? I'm sometimes cold and sometimes hot, but I hope old Father Christmas will never be forgot. Ladies and Gentlemen, I am here for a short time to stay, but I will give you a little pleasure to pass the time, before I go away.

BILLY TWING TWANG: In comes I, little Billy Twing Twang, just come from the press gang. I am not very stout and not very tall, but I think myself the best man amongst you all. Room, room, I pray, for I am the noble Captain to lead King George and all his men this way.

KING GEORGE: In comes I, King George, that man of courage bold. With my broad sword and spear, I won ten tons of gold. I fought the fiery dragon and brought him to great slaughter, and by the means of that I won the King of Egypt's daughter.

TURKISH KNIGHT: In comes I, a Turkish Knight, comes from the Turkish land to fight. I'll fight King George, that man of courage bold. If his blood's hot, I'll quickly turn it cold.

KING GEORGE: Halt, halt, you saucy cock, and don't you talk such vapour, or I'll cut you down with my old rusty rapier.

TURKISH KNIGHT: Down on my bended knee I pray all for to be a Turkish slave, for I've been ragged and I've been jagged from house to house and door to door, and if I get out of this I'll never get in any more.

KING GEORGE: Arise, arise, you Turkish dog, and see that the champion of old England doth remain.

VALIANT SOLDIER: In comes I, a valiant soldier, bold Slasher is my name. With sword and buckle at my side, all to win some fame. I and seven more fought and killed eleven score. Marching men, Sir, men of war, better men than you are. Twice through my head I have been shot, my brains they boil almost like a pot. My head is made of iron, my body made of steel. My sword unto my knuckle bone, I'll fight you in the field. Now broad you stand, you lousy pole, and appear to man as man behold. I will neither bow nor bend, neither will I take you to be my friend. And so that King George should have his will, you, saucy cock, I'd sooner kill.

TURKISH KNIGHT: For why, for why, have I done you any harm?

VALIANT SOLDIER: Yes, you have, you saucy cock, and get you gone.

TURKISH KNIGHT: Saucy cock, Sir? Withdraw your words, you ought to be stabbed.

VALIANT SOLDIER: Stab for stab, I never fear. You point the place and I will meet you there.

TURKISH KNIGHT: Well across the water between four and five, I'll meet you there if I'm alive.

(Here the TURKISH KNIGHT and the VALIANT SOLDIER fight a duel in which the VALIANT SOLDIER kills the TURKISH KNIGHT.)

VALIANT SOLDIER: Now, King George, you can see what I have done. I have cut him down like the evening sun. Now for a doctor you must seek, while he lies bleeding at your feet.

KING GEORGE; Oh, is there a noble doctor to be found, that can do good to raise the sick and heal the wound?

DOCTOR: Yes, there's a doctor to be found that you shall plainly see, as long as I've been doctor on the land and on the sea. Now I've come to behold King George's majesty.

KING GEORGE: Well, doctor, what can you cure?

DOCTOR: What can I cure? I can cure Hippsy, Pippsy, Peasy Palmsy and the Gout, pains within and pains without. Broken arms, broken legs, broken bones of any kind, and if this young man's neck broke, I will set it or I will not charge you one farthing of my fee.

KING GEORGE: And what is your fee, doctor?

DOCTOR: Fifty pounds is my fee, to raise this slain man under thee.

KING GEORGE: Try your skill.

DOCTOR: Try my skill? The Deuce a bit! Get my horse, John, I'll be gone.

KING GEORGE: Step back, doctor, step back. Fifty pounds I'll give thee to raise this slain man under me.

DOCTOR: There, now you talk something like a man. I have a

	little bottle in my pocket called the Golden Lossey Drops. I put one drop on his temple and one on his chin, that's put life in one leg. There, Ladies and Gentlemen, you see it puts life in one leg already. Now, I have some pills here, called reviving pills. I give him one of these and it puts life in his whole body. Now, rise up and see how nobly you can walk and talk.
TURKISH KNIGHT:	There, Ladies and Gentlemen, you see what it is to be slain and have this noble doctor raise you to life again.
DOCTOR:	Yes, Ladies and Gentlemen, I am not like one of those quack doctors, going about from door to door, telling as many lies in half an hour as comes true in seven years. What I do, I do plainly before your eyes and if you can't believe your own eyesight, it is indeed a hard case. My father was the seventh son of his father, and I'll guarantee there is no man can do the cures I can.
THE PRINCE OF PEACE:	In comes I, the Prince of Peace. Bid all these awful wars to cease. So clap your hands together and let your voices ring. Long live King George and merrily we will sing!

⌐   ⌐   ⌐

It may be trite to remark that Christmas is a family holiday, but this was even more true in my mother's and father's time. They both came from families which were large by present-day standards and their pleasures were different from those of today, involving things like home-made crackers, the final visit of the postman on Christmas morning, last-minute shopping until very late on Christmas Eve (or even early on Christmas morning) and, on Christmas afternoon, the family games, in which everyone joined, young and old; and then, on Christmas night, the old songs, some sung only at Christmas. (My grandfather's Christmas song was *The Miner's Dream of Home*.)

Now that the shops close relatively early on Saturdays, it is hard to remember that every Saturday was a miniature Christmas Eve up to the last war. Shops and markets stayed open until eight, nine or even ten o'clock and Saturday-night shopping, with the hope of last-minute reductions, had something of the air of a carnival about it – although possibly not for the poor shop assistant.

As Christmas approached, the shops began to bulge with extra stock, much more apparent in the days of small local businesses than is the case nowadays, when so many shops are large and departmentalised. In particular, the

Above: the Yule Log, always a popular part of Christmas. Even today, people who still have open fires feel impelled to burn logs at Christmas. *Below left:* a country basket-maker. Despite the studio setting on this occasion, he and other such travelling salesmen were once a familiar part of the Sussex countryside. *Below right:* the postman's knock in 1850. Once there were at least three deliveries of mail a day, the post offices were open early and late (and on Sunday mornings) and a letter posted anywhere in Sussex during the day would reach its destination either later that same day or without fail on the following morning.

fishmongers changed their image as Christmas drew near, with vast racks of poultry ready for the shopper. It was common for a shop selling poultry to take another, empty shop nearby just before Christmas, in order to have space to hang the many birds ready for sale.

Traders valued their regular customers enough to give them a little present at Christmastime, and this was expected. From the dairy where I often waited with my mother's white jug, we would receive a small carton of cream; from the little grocer's on the corner, a small box of sweets.

Christmas has for a very long time been commemorated by eating and drinking: and there is plenty of lore about both. As in other counties, we recited:

If the Christmas goose bone be thick,
So will the winter weather be,
If the Christmas goose bone be thin,
So will the winter weather be.

Mince pies are very much a part of our Christmas fare. In Sussex and elsewhere, they were once made in an oval shape, supposedly in imitation of the manger at Bethlehem. Traditionally, the ingredients of mince meat should include minced beef, sultanas, spices, fruit and, in Sussex, smuggled brandy. These were said to represent the gifts of the Three Kings. Mince pies should really only be eaten during the twelve days of Christmas. Every one eaten means a happy month in the following year, provided each one has been made by a different cook. The eating of your first mince pie of the season should be accompanied by a silent wish, as should the stirring of the pudding – a rite in which all the members of the family should be involved. You must not tell anyone your wish, or it will not come true.

Here are two stories about drink at Christmastime. The first is about the organ bellows-blower at Arundel parish church, who arrived for his duties on Christmas Day, 1858, in a very muddled state and, halfway through the service, collapsed on the floor of the organ loft. He recovered sufficiently to carry on but eventually had to be forcibly removed from the church by the sexton and his assistants. As a result, the unfortunate fellow lost his job, which he had held for twenty years.

The second features the workhouse, or 'The Union'. It must have been a cheerless place in the nineteenth century, but efforts were made at Christmas to brighten things up with a little extra food and drink. One newspaper report, dwelling on the good cheer provided at the local workhouse on 25 December, ended with the words, 'A small portion of wholesome beer was allowed.'

In Sussex, as elsewhere, we decorated our houses with evergreens long before the more modern paper-chains made their appearance. Holly and mistletoe were the favourites, holly with as many berries as possible, although

By the middle of the nineteenth century, the railways had almost entirely taken over the carriage of parcels for the Post Office. But in 1887, the four-horse teams and their Royal Mail coaches came back to the roads for a further eighteen years. This is the Royal Parcel Mail Coach, Brighton to London, which made its last journey on 1 June 1905.

An early motor parcel delivery service on the London–Brighton run. It was the last word in modernity at the time.

some years this is difficult. It is said that a year in which the holly trees carry many berries will be a severe one for the birds, although this does not seem to have any foundation in fact.

Mistletoe has a mystic history going back to pre-Christian days (which probably explains why it is not used in church decoration). In Sussex, the fine old custom of kissing a pretty girl under the mistletoe still holds good, although the additional custom of picking off a berry for every kiss is less well known.

Christmas evenings are the proper time to tell ghost stories. There are a great many in Sussex and one would need a whole book to do justice to them all. Brighton is particularly rich in material. One story concerns a ghost called 'Old Strike-a-Light', who inhabited the Rising Sun inn in the eighteenth century, and another the 'Wick Woman', who haunted the gap which formerly ran down to the beach from what is now Langdown Place.

In Horsham, we have – or rather had – a great many ghosts. Some were connected with St Leonards Forest, where smugglers operated. For obvious reasons, smugglers and ghosts often go together, as the former made use of local stories and legends to keep law-abiding folk away from the scenes of their nocturnal activities.

One lady has learned to live with her ghost, who inhabits a room of her small but ancient house. She treats him with tolerant amusement, giving him a Christian name and refusing to be frightened even when he brushes past her on the narrow staircase leading to his room or when the temperature drops suddenly in the room itself.

◇　◇　◇

The pleasant custom of carol singing is very popular today. In the past, it was sometimes called wassailing (not to be confused with the New Year custom of wassailing the trees). At one time, children went round the houses with a miniature cradle and a doll representing the Christ child. The rhyme which went with this custom was:

> *I wish you a merry Christmas*
> *And a happy New Year,*
> *A pocketful of money*
> *And a barrel full of beer.*

Other beliefs connected with Christmas included the one that the Christmas tree, when its life indoors was over, should not be planted in the garden, otherwise as the tree thrived so the child would sicken; and the weather was foretold by the saying, 'Balcony Christmas, fireside Easter'.

Traditionally, Christmas should have snow, although in fact the hardest weather usually comes well afterwards: 'as the days lengthen, so the cold strengthens.' In December 1836, however, there was a very heavy fall of snow

In the days before frozen chickens, any kind of poultry for Sunday dinner was a very rare treat. In our family, it was enjoyed only on Christmas Day. Plucking and preparing the bird was usually done at home, preceded, if it was a backyard chicken, by the killing of the victim. My mother remembered one of her brothers running amok with an axe and decapitating chickens in the yard right, left and centre. His defence was that he was only doing what he had seen his father do.

Mr Jarvis and Mr Jones, the village butchers at Etchingham, fully prepared for the Christmas rush. The year is 1910.

in Sussex. On the morning of 27 December, a great mass fell on some cottages from the hills near Lewes, demolishing the cottages and killing eight people, including a girl of eleven and a man of eighty-two. The sad event was marked by a poem written by Richard Tugwell, of Lewes, who described himself simply as a working man:

The people of Lewes, they long will remember
The huge drift of snow that fell in December.
At Christmas it fell and lay in great heaps,
And there was no passing about in the streets.
The high roads were stopped to the neighbouring towns,
The snow was destruction that hung on the Downs.
At the end of South Street, that leads out of town,
Seven houses the snow completely knocked down –
And, ruined, fifteen poor creatures there lay,
And eight of them dead, we lament for to say:
Two lads, each of them with their legs sadly broke,
And five taken out unhurt by the stroke.
It was very distressing to see and to hear them,
The screams of their friends awaiting to see them:
Their furniture broke and their little all gone,
But kind friends to help were all over town:
A subscription was raised to help their distress,
Their labour God has most wonderfully blest.

Not good poetry, but vivid reporting. Presumably, the final line meant the kind folk who organised the subscription.

Food for Christmas

To conclude, a few Christmas recipes and others for special occasions:

CHRISTMAS CAKE

$\frac{1}{2}$ lb good beef dripping	$\frac{1}{2}$ lb raisins, stoned and chopped
$\frac{1}{2}$ lb brown sugar	$\frac{1}{4}$ lb chopped mixed peel
4 eggs	2 oz shredded almonds
10 oz flour	1 large lemon
Pinch salt	$\frac{1}{2}$ teaspoon baking powder
Pinch spice	Milk
$\frac{1}{2}$ lb currants	2 tablespoons brandy

The old cannon which each New Year's Eve at Warnham Court heralds the arrival of another year. The custom is relatively modern: it was started in the nineteenth century by the Lucas family. In 1977, the customary twelve rounds failed to sound, because the estate foreman, who was loading the cannon, received injuries to his hands when the charge ignited and blew out the ram rod, the first accident of its kind. *(Photograph: West Sussex County Times.)*

Desolate Eastbourne after the Great Blizzard of 1908. Sussex usually enjoys much less severe winters than many counties.

Slightly melt the beef dripping and beat it to a cream with the brown sugar. Add the four eggs, well beaten, and beat again. Stir in the flour, the pinch of salt and a good pinch of spice. Add the currants and raisins, the mixed peel and the shredded almonds, plus the juice of one large lemon. Mix well. Stir in half teaspoon of baking powder dissolved in a little milk. Last of all, stir in the two tablespoons of brandy. Beat again for at least 15 minutes. Pour into a tin lined with greased paper and bake in a moderate oven for about 4 hours.

(From Miss L. N. Candlin, of Brighton. This was her grandmother's recipe. She called it her 'Christmas biscuit'. Up to the nineteenth century, the words 'cake' and 'biscuit' seem to have been interchangeable in Sussex.)

SUSSEX MINCEMEAT

$\frac{1}{2}$ *lb lean beef (well boiled)*	*2 oz candied peel*
$\frac{1}{2}$ *lb beef suet*	*6 apples*
$\frac{1}{4}$ *lb sugar*	*Nutmeg*
$\frac{1}{2}$ *lb currants*	*Brandy*

Cut up the beef and apples very small and mix with the other ingredients. The mince pies should be oval shaped (the traditional shape of a mince pie in Sussex).

(From S. Land, of Storrington.)

GINGERBREAD

The annual fairs in Horsham were once famous for gingerbread, sometimes sold in the shape of popular characters – Wellington, for example.

$\frac{1}{2}$ *lb self-raising flour*	*1 teaspoon ground ginger*
3 tablespoons golden syrup	*1 teaspoon bicarbonate of soda*

Mix the flour and golden syrup together in a basin. Mix the ground ginger and bicarbonate of soda in a cup with tepid water. Add this to the contents of the basin and stir well until the mixture is runny. Turn into well-greased, flat tin and bake in a moderate oven for $1\frac{1}{4}$ hours.

PARTRIDGE PUDDING

Suet dough	*Parsley*
Joints of partridge	*Thyme*
Flour	*Glass of sherry*
Lean pork, cut into squares	*Gravy stock*
Prunes	

Line a basin with suet dough (as for a steak-and-kidney pudding). Fill with the joints of partridge (rolled in seasoned flour), squares of lean pork and stoned prunes. Flavour with chopped parsley and fresh thyme. Moisten with a

Five Sussex characters of the early 1900s. *Top left:* Thomas Friend, born in 1836, is seen at 85 carrying home fuel for his winter fire. *Top right:* Horsham's 'Champion Town Crier of the United Kingdom', William Law. *Bottom left:* the Wheeler Band (all two of them), of Brighton, a town once noted for its many street musicians. *Bottom right:* Charles Andrew, who was known, however lugubrious he may look in this picture, as 'The Brighton Jester'.

glass of sherry and stock. Cover with suet dough top. Cook as for a meat pudding.

SIMPLE SHORTBREAD

3 tablespoons self raising flour
1 tablespoon sugar   *2 oz margarine*

Cream margarine and sugar together and work in flour. Roll and knead into a flat round. Pinch up edges with finger, prick all over with a fork, make into sections and bake on a greased tin in a slow oven (electric 375) until firm – about 20 minutes.

APPLE MARMALADE

3 lb apples (after peeling and coring)   *2 oz fine shredded candied peel*
1 pint water   *1 lemon*
                                           4 lb sugar

Cut the apples into small pieces. Put into a pan with the water, the peel and the grated rind and juice of the lemon. Simmer until soft, then add sugar. Stir while it dissolves, and cook on until the marmalade is thick.

ROSE-PETAL JAM

Rose petals $\frac{1}{2}$ *lb sugar*
Lemon juice $\frac{1}{2}$ *lb honey*

Gather rose petals over 2–3 days, putting them into a deep crock. Squeeze a little lemon juice over them as you go along. Keep crock covered. When you have enough, allow $\frac{1}{2}$ lb sugar and $\frac{1}{2}$ lb honey to each pound of petals. Add a very little water, then boil gently till jam sets.

(From E. Tucker, of Brighton.)

GINGER-
-BREAD.

References and Bibliography

Albery, William. *A Millennium of Facts in the History of Horsham and Sussex*, 1947
— *A Parliamentary History of Horsham*, 1927
Allcroft, A. Hadrian. *Downland Pathways*, 1924
Axon, W. E. A. *Bygone Sussex*, 1897
Baker, Michael. *Sussex Villages*, 1977
Barr-Hamilton, Alec. *In Saxon Sussex*
Barty-King, Hugh. *Sussex in 1839*, 1974
Beckett, Arthur. *Adventures of a Quiet Man*, 1933
— *The Spirit of the Downs*, 1909
— *The Wonderful Weald*, 1924
Blaker, N. P. *Sussex in Bygone Days*, 1919
Brabant, F. G. *Rambles in Sussex*, 1909
Broadwood, Lucy E. *English County Songs*
— *English Traditional Songs and Carols*, 1912
Burstow, Henry. *Reminiscences of Horsham*, 1911 and 1975
Butterworth, George. *Folk Songs from Sussex*, 1912
Cobbett, Martin. *Wayfaring Notions*, 1906
Cook, W. Victor. *The Story of Sussex*, 1920
Cooper, William Durrant. *A Glossary of the Provincialisms in Use in the County of Sussex*, 1853
Cooper, William. *Smuggling in Sussex*, 1858
Copper, Bob. *A Song for Every Season*, 1971
— *Songs and Southern Breezes*, 1973
— *Early to Rise*, 1976
Crookshank, A. C. *St Leonard of Sussex*
Darby, Ben. *The South Downs*, 1976
— *View of Sussex*, 1975
Day, Alice Catharine. *Glimpses of Rural Life in Sussex*
Done, W. E. P. *Looking Back in Sussex*, 1953
Dudley, Howard. *The History and Antiquities of Horsham*, 1836
Egerton, Rev. J. Coker. *Sussex Folk and Sussex Ways*, 1892
Ellman, Rev. Edward Boys. *Recollections of a Sussex Parson*, 1925
Evans, A. A. *By Weald and Down*, 1939
— *On Foot in Sussex*, 1933
— *A Saunterer in Sussex*, 1933
Fleet, C. *Glimpses of Our Sussex Ancestors*, vols. 1 and 2, 1882–3
Geering, Thomas. *Our Sussex Parish*, 1925
Gill, W. H. *Songs of the British Folk*, 1917

Gosset, Adelaide and L. J. *Shepherds of Britain*, 1911
Green, Andrew. *Ghosts of the South East*, 1976
Green, F. E. *The Tyranny of the Countryside*, 1913
Hannah, Ian C. *The Sussex Coast*, 1912
Harper, C. G. *The Brighton Road*, 1892
Harrison, Frederick. *Notes on Sussex Churches*, 1920
Hay, David and Joan. *The Downs from the Sea*, 1972
Hopkins, R. Thurston. *Kipling's Sussex*, 1924
 — *Kipling's Sussex Revisited*, 1928
 — *The Lure of Sussex*, 1928
 — *Sussex Rendezvous*
 — *Sussex Pilgrimage*, 1927
Hudson, W. H. *Nature in Downland*, 1900
Hurst, Dorothea E. *Horsham, Its History and Antiquities*, 1868
 — *The History and Antiquities of Horsham*, 1889
Jennings, Louis J. *Field Paths and Green Lanes*, 1877
Leigh, Rhode. *Past and Passing*, 1932
Lewis, Ralph. *Scene in Sussex*
Lower, Mark Anthony. *Contributions to Literature*
Lower, Richard. *Jan Cladpole's Trip to 'Merricur in Search of Dollar Trees*
 — *Tom Cladpole's Jurney to Lunnon*
Lucas, E. V. *Highways and Byways in Sussex*, 1919
Macdermott, K. H. *Sussex Church Music in the Past*, 1922
Mais, S. P. B. *It Isn't Far from London*, 1930
 — *Sussex*, 1929
Martin, E. A. *Life in a Sussex Windmill*, 1921
Maxwell, Donald. *A Detective in Sussex*, 1932
Merrick, W. Percy. *Folk Songs from Sussex*, 1912
Meynell, Esther. *Country Ways*, 1942
 — *Small Talk in Sussex*, 1954
 — *Sussex*
 — *Sussex Cottage*, 1936
Mee, Arthur. *Sussex*, 1937
Morris, John, ed. *Domesday Book – Sussex*, 1976
Mundy, Percy D. *Memorials of Old Sussex*, 1909
Musgrave, Clifford. *Sussex*, 1957
Neale, Kenneth. *Victorian Horsham*, 1975
Paddon, J. B. *Sequestered Vales of Sussex*
Parish, W. D. *A Dictionary of the Sussex Dialect*, 1875
Peat, A. H. and Halstead, L. C. *Churches and Other Antiquities of West Sussex*, 1912
Price, Bernard. *Sussex* (People-Places-Things), 1975

Rees, Arthur. *Old Sussex and Her Diarists*, 1929
Robinson, Maude. *A Southdown Farm in the Sixties*, 1947
Rudkin, Mabel. *Seeing Sussex*, 1930
Rush, Philip. *Great Men of Sussex*, 1956
Scott, Hardiman. *Secret Sussex*, 1949
Simpson, Jacqueline. *The Folklore of Sussex*, 1973
Anon. *Smuggling and Smugglers in Sussex*
Summers, A. Leonard. *Southern Sketch-Book*, 1921
Anon. *Sussex Industries*, 1883
Sussex Archaeological Collections
Sussex County Magazines
Sussex Life
Sussex Notes and Queries
Taylor, James. *The Sussex Garland*, 1851
Thomson, W. *The Avalanche at Lewes*, 1892
West Sussex County Times
West Sussex Gazette
White, Gilbert. *The Natural History of Selborne*, 1788
White, Iris Bryson. *Sussex Crafts*, 1974
White, John Talbot. *The South-East*, 1977
Wills, Barclay. *Downland Treasure*, 1929
   — *Bypaths in Downland*, 1927
   — *Shepherds of Sussex*, 1938
Wolseley, Viscountess. *The Countryman's Log Book*, 1921
   — *Some Sussex Byways*, 1930
Wood, William. *A Sussex Farmer*, 1938
Woodford, Cecile. *Portrait of Sussex*, 1972
Woodward, Marcus. *The Mistress of Stanton's Farm*, 1938
Wymer, Norman. *Companion into Sussex*, 1972
Wyndham, Margaret. *Mrs Paddick*, 1947

Also many local town and village histories.

Index

Figures in italic refer to illustrations: they indicate either the page on, or the page opposite, which an illustration appears.

'A-goodening', 100
ALCISTON, 28, *68*
ALFRISTON, 96
Aldridge, R., 100
AMBERLEY, *12*, *62*
Andrew, Charles, 116
ARUNDEL, 110
Attrill, George, 65, 68, 104

BALCOMBE, *38*
BALCOMBE FOREST, *18*
BARNHAM, *32*, 70
BARNS GREEN, 48
BATTLE, 28, *44*
Battle of Agincourt, 74
BEEDING, 50
Belton, George, 68
Bees, 20
BEXHILL, *56*
BILLINGSHURST, 28, 88
BISHOPSTONE, 14
Blacksmiths, 87, *96*
Blann, Michael, 68
BOGNOR REGIS, *56*, *58*, 60
Bonfire Boys, 87
Bonfire societies, 87
Boxing Day, 16, 100, 104
BOXGROVE, 104
BRAMBER, *16*
BRIGHTON, 28, 54, *58*, *60*, *82*, 87, *88*, 90, 112, *116*
Broadwood, Lucy, 16, 102, 104
Broadwood Morris Men, 16, 18, 104
BUCKS GREEN, *88*
BURGESS HILL, *68*
BURPHAM, 14
Burstow, Henry, 16, 94, 100

CABURN, MT, *48*
Candlemass Day, 22
Carols, 102
Carters, 16, 72
Catt, Mr, 14
'Catterning and Clemening', 90
CHAILEY GREEN, *96*
CHANCTONBURY RING, 50
Chanctonbury Ring Morris Men, 18, 104
Charcoal burners, *18*

Charles II, 44
Charms, 90
CHICHESTER, 43, 68
CHIDDINGLY, 94
Christmas, 16, 100, 108
CLAYTON, *30*
Clubs, 44
Cobbs Mill, *14*
Cock fighting, 28
Cock throwing, 28
Collinson, Francis, 52
Cook, Victor, 11
COOLHAM, *74*
Cooper, Margaret, 90
CRAWLEY, 14, *22*, *30*
Crowborough Fair, 27
Cuckoos, 27
'Cuckoo Day', 27

Dancing, 52
Death, 18
'Degradation of Drunkenness', 74
DEVIL'S DYKE, 38
Dialect, 76
'DIDLING HARBOUR', 80
DOWNS, THE, 28
Drinking, 65
Duke, Blake, 14
Duke, Newall, 14
DUNCTON, 18

EASTBOURNE, 22, *114*
Easter Day, 32
EBERNOE, 52
Egg rolling, 28
ETCHINGHAM, *112*
Evershed, Rev. P., 28

Fairies, 50
FALMER, *50*, *82*
FAYGATE, 80
Fire, 58
'Firing the anvil', 90
FIRLE, 96
Fishermen, 28, *38*, 40, 44
FITTLEWORTH, 65, 104, 106
Fleas, 27
Foresters, *20*

Fox, Mrs, 100
Friend, Thomas, 116
Friendly societies, 44

'Garland Day', 43
Garlands, 43
Garson, Dame, 90
Ghosts, 112
Godsmark, Thomas, *68*
Good Friday, 28
'Gooding Day', 100
Goodyer, George, 14
Graburn, Lawrie, 14
Grottoes, 54
Guy Fawkes Night, 87

HAILSHAM, 18
Halloween, 74
Hare hunting, 22
HARTING, 46
Harvest suppers, 65
HASTINGS, *38, 40*
Heathfield Fair, 27
'Heffel Cuckoo Day', 27
HENFIELD, *22*
Hessel, Phoebe, 100, *102*
HICKSTEAD, *78*
Hoops, *28*, 32
Horn Fair, 52,
HORSHAM, 12, 14, *20*, 30, 44, *76*, *80*, 87, 90,
    94, 100, *100*, 102, 104, 112, *116*
HORSTED KEYNES, *102*
Hot cross buns, 28
HOVE, 28
Howling, 18
Howling Boys, 18

IDEN, *46*
ITCHINGFIELD, 48

Kensett, Miss, 14
King, E., 70
King George and the Dragon, 104, 106
KINGSFOLD, 52, *52*
KIRDFORD, 16, 74, *78*, 88, 90
'Kiss in the Ring', 52
Knight, Richard (Spratty), 18
Knight, William, 18

Laker, Mr, 87
Law, William, *116*
Lent, 28
LEWES, 14, 76, 87, 114
Lifeboats, *22*
LITTLEHAMPTON, *54*

'Long Man of Wilmington,
    The', *62*, 96
'Long Rope (or Line) Day', 28
Lower, Richard, 94
LULLINGTON, *32*
LYMINSTER, 14

MADEHURST, 68
Mafeking Night, 88
'Marble Day', 28
Marbles, 28, *28*
Marriage, 18, 54
May Day, 43
Maynard, George (Pop), 30
Midsummer, 50
Miner's Dream of Home, 108
Morris men, 16, 18, 102, 104
Mumming plays, 102

New Year, 16, 20, 104, *114*
NEWHAVEN, 28
Noelle, Donald R., 46
NORTHIAM, 46, *74*

'Oak Apple Day', 44
Old Clem, 87
On Christmas Night all Christians sing, 102
Orange rolling, 28
Oxen, *34, 68*

'PALLINGHAM QUAY', 80
PATCHAM, 80
Perigoe, Mrs Nellie, 46
PETWORTH, 24, 43
Phillips, Cyril, 96
'Pinching Day', 44
POOK HALE, 50
POOK HOLE, 50
POOK-RYDE, 50
POOKBOURNE, 50
Potter, Stephen, 12
Pound Day, 18
PRESTON, 32
POYNINGS, *96*
PUCK'S CHURCH PARLOUR, 50
PULBOROUGH, 70
PYECOMBE, 90

Quoits, *104*

Religion, 34, 56
RINGMER, *20, 48*
Rotary, 102
ROTTINGDEAN, *28*, 68
RUSPER, 16, 80, 102, 104

St Bartholemew's Day, 54
St Catherine's Day, 90
St Clement's Day, 87
St Crispin's Day, 74
St George and the Turk, 102
St James's Day, 52
ST LEONARD'S, 100
ST LEONARD'S FOREST, 100
St Paul's Day, 22
St Swithin's Day, 52
St Thomas's Day, 100
St Valentine's Day, 22
SELMESTON, *104*
Sheep-shearing, 46
Shelley, Sir Thomas, 100
SHOREHAM, 28, 43
Shrove Tuesday, 28
Skipping, 28
Skittles, 28
SLAUGHAM, 14, 74
SLINFOLD, *96*
Smallwood, Mrs, 44
Smocks, 14
Smugglers, 50
SOUTH HARTING, 46
SOUTHWATER, 24, *30*
STAPLEFIELD, *46*, *104 (cap.)*
STEYNING, 76, 104
STORRINGTON, 87, 88
Street rhymes, 32
Superstitions, 56
SUSSEX
– carols, 102
– character, 11
– humour, 92

– mud, 24
- roads, 16
– tall tales, 94
Sussex Toast, 68

Tester, Scan, *102*
Tipteers, 102, *104*
TINSLEY GREEN, 28
Toasts, 68
Townsend, George, *34 (cap.)*, 87
Tredcroft, Mrs, 44
Trug basket, *74*
Twelfth Night, 100

Vaughan Williams, Ralph, 52, 102
Verralls, The, 102
Voice, Mr, *76*

Walpole, Horace, 24
WARNHAM, 16, *16*, *52*, *114*
Wassailing, 16, 112
WEST CHILTINGTON, *28*, 70
WEST GRINSTEAD, 70
West Sussex Gazette, 102
Wheeler Band, The, *116*
Whitmonday, 44
Windmills, 30, 32
WISBOROUGH GREEN, 34
Witches, 90
Woods, Miss Faith, 11
WORTHING, 52, 68, 88

YAPTON, 80, *80*
Yule Log, The, 100, *108*

Index to recipes

Acres Pudding, 24
Apple Marmalade, 18
Apple Turnover, 64

Balm Wine, 99
Beetroot Wine, 98
Blackeyed Susan, 80
Bolster (or Blanket)
    Pudding, 25

Chiddingly Hot Pot, 85
Christmas Cake, 114
Cider Wine, 98
Claversham Rissoles, 40
Coager Cake, 86

Donkey Tea, 99

Elderberry Wine, 96

FOOD FOR CHRISTMAS, 114
Fried Mackerel, 40

Gingerbread, 116
Grilled Mackerel, 40

Hard Dumplings, 84
Hastings Gurnet, 40
Hasty Pudding, 25
Herb Pie, 62
Huckle-My-Bluff, 99

Lardy Johns, 86

Mackerel Pudding, 26
Marrow Stew, 42
MEAT, FISH AND SAVOURY DISHES, 38
Military Pudding, 25

Nettle Beer, 99

Old-fashioned Bread Pudding, 24
Old Sussex Potato and Cheese Cakes, 40

Partridge Pudding, 116
PIES, 60
Potato Wine, 96
Pumpkin Pie, 60
PUDDINGS, 24

Rice and Apple Pudding, 26
Rose-petal Jam, 118

Simple Shortbread, 118
Soused Mackerel, 42
Sussex Bacon Pudding No. 1, 84
    – No. 2, 85
Sussex Cakes, 86
Sussex Currant and Apple Dumplings, 86
Sussex Dripped Pudding, 80
Sussex Fritters, 38
Sussex Meat Pudding, 84
Sussex Mincemeat, 116
Sussex Mock Pork Pie, 64
Sussex Plum Heavies, 82
Sussex Pudding, 26
Sussex Pond Pudding, 82
Sussex Savoury Dumplings, 84
SUSSEX WINES AND OTHER DRINKS, 96
Swimmers, 26
Syllabub, 99

Ten-to-One Pie, 62
Tomato Pie, 62
TRADITIONAL SUSSEX DISHES, 80
Treacle Beer, 98

Vegetable Pie, 62

Well Pudding, 80
Windmill Hill Thin Biscuits, 85